D1474672

Keys to Brilliant Focus

The Power of Wisdom to Reclaim Your Identity

by Graham Cooke

The Wisdom Series — Book Three

Brilliant
BOOK HOUSE

www.BrilliantBookHouse.com

Wisdom that stretches our thinking and enlarges our heart.

A book of aphorisms by Graham Cooke.

Brilliant Book House LLC
1498 SE Tech Center Pl, Ste 120
Vancouver, WA 98683
USA

www.brilliantbookhouse.com

©2012 Graham Cooke & Brilliant Book House

Unless otherwise indicated, all Scripture quotations are taken from The Holy Bible, New King James Version (Copyright © 1979, 1980, 1982 by Thomas Nelson, Inc.) and the New American Standard Bible (Copyright © 1960, 1962, 1963, 1971, 1972, 1973, 1975, 1977, 1995 by The Lockman Foundation).

Requests for information should be addressed to:

Graham Cooke
office@brilliantperspectives.com

ISBN 978-1-934771-23-5

Dedication

To all people everywhere who are embarking on a new life. Whether you are breaking out of habitual circumstances or breaking into a new identity in Christ.

You may be trying something new or simply re-ordering your private world. In life every relationship we have must reinvent itself every 3–5 years, or grow stale and cold over time.

New dreams come, passions are upgraded and old longings come to fruition. Every scenario of life will demand fresh faith, favor and focus.

I dedicate this book to all seekers everywhere. May this be the year of your rising!

TABLE OF CONTENTS

Acknowledgements

True friends are those who walk in when others are walking away. Real friends hold your truth in their hearts and speak it to you so that you have something to embrace when you want to quit. Good friends celebrate you when you feel unworthy. Great friends defend you to the death when you are at your most stupid.

Amazing friends stand the test of faithfulness so that you can see God in the dark.

Love never fails. It bids you stand on its shoulders and reach into the next level of your destiny.

I have friends like these. I am truly blessed.

A note on meditation

The purpose of this book is to lead you out of the busyness of life and into the still waters of deep thought, restful perception and therefore *presence*. As you give yourself to this process you will become more God-conscious, more of a worshipper, and more peaceful in how you approach life.

To meditate means to think deeply about something or someone. It means to explore with mind and heart, allowing what you think to touch your innermost being.

Meditation is creative thought which leads us to a higher realm of revelation and wisdom. It takes us beyond the place of reason to where joy is seated and faith is activated.

Meditation allows us to search inside and outside the box of our current paradigm. What you see and hear there touches you profoundly. It adds a ring around the core truth of Christ, which is God within, the certainty of freedom.

Fruitful meditation is therefore not a casual seeking for revelatory insight. Initial creative thoughts are merely the "X" that marks the spot. There is treasure in meditation, a guarantee of wealth in the pursuit of God.

Many are satisfied with collecting random truth on the surface of their consciousness. It is good, wholesome stuff, but it does not satisfy and it cannot challenge the complexities of life in a warfare context.

Deep truth has to be mined over days and weeks. It takes joy and patience to take truth down to its deepest level. Beyond meeting our current needs, beyond the depth of understanding the power, it releases to us against our adversary. Down to the depth where God lives in the highest places of heaven. For all meditation must ultimately come before the throne of His majesty, sovereignty and supremacy. He fills all things with Himself.

Our current situation requires wisdom, but even more it yearns for presence. Meditation allows us to experience both, through the word coming alive in our spirit. Meditation leads us to God and the permission of His heart. Learn to be in the question peacefully with God. Let the Holy Spirit teach you how to abide. Turn inwardly and rest; wait patiently… He will come. When your heart gets restless, turn to worship. When the interior atmosphere settles, return to listening.

Write down initial thoughts, but do not pursue them just yet. Do not be distracted by what you hear initially; set it aside, come back to it later.

When first entering a lifestyle of meditation, take care to ease into it slowly. An hour at first, then longer until half a day and so on.

Always have a focus; do not try to wait in a vacuum. In this book are a series of sayings and life statements. Take time to process them. Enjoy the stillness of deep thinking and allow your heart to flow in and out of worship.

Use the questions as the Spirit leads. They are not prescriptive but merely a guide to enable your contemplation. No doubt you will discover better questions as the Holy Spirit tutors you.

Enjoy!

About Personal Notes

Following each entry, you will find blank or mostly blank pages like this one to help you in your journaling. Each of these has a question or questions to help direct you in your meditation. They can be used or ignored; they are merely there as a starting point or guide. These "Personal Notes" sections have been included so you may write His thoughts and keep them close.

Dear Reader:
I have deliberately not
expounded on some
concepts... the Holy
Spirit will have that
pleasure Himself.
Just ask!

Heaven is attracted to Jesus in you

One of the greatest ideas of the Father was to put us into Jesus and Jesus into us. The Father and Jesus love to make their abode in us (John 14:23).

We are the residence of God and as we are empowered by the Holy Spirit to love Jesus and keep His words, then heaven dwells within us and we become highly attractive in the Kingdom.

If we are in Christ then heaven's fascination with Him makes our life extremely interesting. We are learning to pay attention to Jesus because all our freedoms flow from that direction. This is why we are not to be caught out dealing with the old nature. We are not pastoring someone who God has already deemed to be dead (Romans 6:11). That would be like baby-sitting a corpse!

"If we have died with Him we believe that we will also live with Him" (Romans 6:8). We are walking in newness of life learning to be alive only to God (Romans 6). We are therefore not declaring what we are not, but proclaiming who we are in Jesus.

No one can be ordinary when they are in Jesus. It is not allowed! Heaven comes to us because of our placement in Jesus, not because of our performance as believers.

Take a few moments to really imagine what it feels like to have Jesus reside in you. Ask for His perspective on that part of your life that needs an upgrade.

Ask Him to show you what He is seeing and thinking about you in Him. Relax into a place of thanks and rejoice in His presence. Record the outcome that heaven opens up to you.

Make yourself vulnerable to God

Because we are in Jesus and He is in us, we are learning the lifestyle of the power of THE ONE with the one. Jesus is the catalyst for all our spiritual development. "In Him we live, and move and have our being" (Acts 17:28).

That means we are completely open to all the fullness of God in Christ Jesus. "Of His fullness have we all received, and grace upon grace" (John 1:16). Our goal in life with God is to reach such a saturation point that as God continues to pour Himself out on us so we overflow to all around us.

Fullness denotes a profusion of life, blessing and favor. Enough for ourselves and the people group to whom we are sent. It depicts a completion, a wholeness, and extensiveness in the loving-kindness of God that compels people to know Him. We become His visual aid in the Kingdom. We resonate with His voice in the earth. We, His body, demonstrate His abundance in all our earthly connections (Ephesians 1:23).

We come to the place of absolute truth as we learn to know the love of Christ, which surpasses knowledge, and are filled up to all the fullness of God (Ephesians 3:19). It is our daily privilege to make ourselves vulnerable to God's fullness, knowing that He loves to fill all in all with Himself. Whatever we need to become like Christ is fully accessible and available only in fullness. Christ is applicable everywhere, every time. When we make ourselves vulnerable to God's passion for us, then our delight in Him is the fruit. We learn the joy of attending on God.

One person plus God has all the power and authority necessary to overcome. We are vulnerable to the Christ within. We are not vulnerable to the enemy at all, unless we choose to be.

If Heaven represents the fullness of Christ in you, how does that change your perspective, thinking and language about who He is in you and who you are in Him?

What are you currently making yourself vulnerable to in your life circumstances? Are you readily available for worry, fear, anxiety, believing the worst? How does that affect your trust, faith and giving thanks? The opposite of that is what you make yourself sensitive and open towards. We are wide open to grace. Practice making yourself vulnerable to goodness.

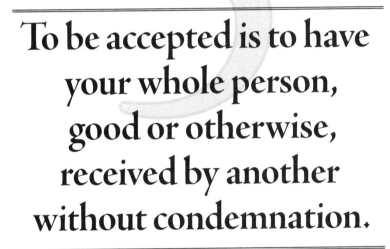

To be accepted is to have
your whole person,
good or otherwise,
received by another
without condemnation.

God has made us accepted in the Beloved (Ephesians 1:3–9). We are told to "accept one another just as Christ also accepted you, to the glory of God." (Romans 15:7)

Acceptance is to receive someone into relationship. Love God wholeheartedly and love your neighbor as yourself.

What does the word acceptance mean to you? What must change in you to practice a lifestyle of acceptance with no thought of condemnation, judgment or criticism?

To practice your delight
you must first turn it all on Jesus

There are no disciplines in heaven. No one is standing around the throne, looking at their watch and gritting their teeth to get through the discipline of worship.

In Christ we make His passions our own with the help of the incomparable Holy Spirit. In Christ all our disciplines must become delights. Life in the Spirit can never be separated from joy (John 15:11).

Delight is the enjoyment of gladness. It lies in practicing the gleeful spirit of someone captivated by Jesus. Rejoicing is the art of being cheerful in tribulation because of the majesty of God. When we are overwhelmed by the beauty of Christ it is hard to be overcome by anything else.

To love consistently we must focus our attention from the heart. Our hidden person of the heart (1 Peter 3:4) is learning to flow in the nature of God. We move in the fruit of the Spirit, the very nature of God. We are filled with Christ so naturally He becomes our full focus for life. We learn the lifestyle of spirituality by remaining fixed on the architect of it all, Jesus. He is the author and the finisher of our faith outcome (Hebrew 12:2).

When we allow His affection for us to overwhelm us, He becomes the object of our desire.

When we receive His joy over us our rejoicing increases. When we accept His passion for us we love Him with all our heart.

God delights in me and as I bask in His acceptance and pleasure, my delight in Him grows. Love begets love. Joy produces joy. Delight establishes delight.

God delights in Christ in us. We receive that delight as our own and return it back to Him by rejoicing and thanksgiving. God's pleasure in us must be reciprocated through us and returned to Him (Romans 11:35–36). It is the cycle of spirituality.

What passion have you received from the Lord? Practice them joyfully back to Him. Allow them to touch others on their way back to God.

What areas of your life need some new delight? Talk to the happy God who loves Jesus in you and receive some truth, revelation and wisdom that will lead you into a fresh encounter with God and an ongoing experience for life.

Proclamation on this level is the key to the next

In the Spirit we must talk our way into everything. What we believe must be spoken aloud into the atmosphere of our circumstances. We speak from the inner man of the spirit into the outer world of our life situation. Faith comes by hearing and confession, declaration and proclamation are vital in the ongoing battle to govern in our circumstances.

We confess what God has said about our circumstances. We declare to the enemy who we are in Christ in this particular situation. We proclaim to the Lord in thanksgiving who He is for us in the scenario in which we are involved.

If the voice of our inner man* is stilled, the voice of our outer man of the soul will be heard.

Our inner man only lives in the presence of God and can only hear His voice. The outer man of the soul is more in tune with the world around us and is susceptible to any negative voice, information and perception. These can have a dissenting and opposing effect on our spirituality.

Life in the Spirit is concerned with the art of abiding in Christ. Our proclamation of who God is for us goes hand in hand with His perceptions of our identity on this level. As we live and move in that identity it is firmly established by what we speak and how we act on that. Continuous proclamation opens us up to the upgrade the Father has designed for us. When we prove out on this level the next level comes into view and the whole joyful process begins again but higher up.

Through prophecy and the inheritance words of scripture we are awakened to the next level of our upgrade in identity. In confession we learn how to live in the circumstances. In declaration we master how to stand in opposition to the enemy. In proclamation we embrace the identity and the resources that come to us through the Lord Jesus.

---

*See *Towards a Powerful Inner Life* for truth regarding soul and spirit.

Personal Notes

At this time what are you confessing, declaring and proclaiming? What promises have been spoken to you in the prophetic or through scripture? What belongs to you on this current level?

Speak it out. A voice will be heard in your present life circumstance. Will it be from your spirit or your soul?

Always start with your future, not your present

It is so very easy to become dismayed about the future. It can seem so out of focus or out of reach. One reason for that lack of clarity is that we are discouraged about who we are in the present. We can lack the fortitude to move forward because our identity needs an upgrade in the here and now.

God uses scripture in a personal and relational way with His people. He is part of our story and journey. We belong to Him and must walk with Him in the way of his choosing. He gives us passages of scripture because He wants them to give us vision and inspire our identity.

He gives us promises that He intends to be realized in our life circumstances.

Several decades ago He gave me Numbers chapters 13 and 14; the story of Caleb. When the Lord gives you scripture with some-one's name in it, He intends that you will have a similar encounter and experience of Him that this particular individual enjoyed. Caleb became "a man of a different spirit" from those around him, a stand-out person both in his own tribe and to successive generations of Israelites.

I have sought to partner with the Holy Spirit in the cultivation of that identity. My outlook on life, problems, difficulties and warfare stem from the sense of majesty that Caleb obviously adored.

Our vision of the future must have an impact on who we are now. We are in Christ who is our prophet, priest and king. Therefore the prophetic part of His nature empowers us to interact with our future as we relate to God in the present. That means in prayer and devotion we can explore the plans of God now in fellowship. We can go into the future in our sanctified imagination and dream of what the Lord is seeing, thinking, planning and speaking. We can get a sense of how it looks and feels to be in that place of favor.

In Exodus 7:1, God invites Moses to: "See, I have made you as God to Pharaoh and Aaron shall be your prophet." What an amazing invitation to explore the future and bring back the identity required to go there in the present!!

Moses got to travel over the ground he would have to take within himself so that he could stand before Pharaoh with an authority and majesty greater than this earthly ruler possessed. This is where we learn to partner with the Holy Spirit who takes what belongs to Jesus for us, and makes it real in us. (John 16:15) So, then, we are made in His specific image according to the call on our lives in the Kingdom.

The future is designed to make our present become brilliant. Prophecy achieves the same purpose. God speaks from the future into our present so that we have a clear path to go there in fellowship with Him. Prophecy gives us an outcome, which means that from prophecy spoken to prophecy fulfilled, everything between those two places is now designed to train us to become the person God saw when He spoke over us. The process to fulfillment is our training and proving ground where we cultivate the identity and develop the faith, focus and favor required to move in the Spirit at that level.*

Our problem can be that we have a limited vision of our identity (who we are in God's eyes) in the present. That is precisely why God speaks to us. He must upgrade our vision to His. We learn to view where we stand in relation to where we are going. We learn to comprehend how to stand in relation to who we are becoming.

Everything begins and ends with God. He is both the Author and the Finisher (Hebrews 12:2) of our faith. That means the outline of our story is established in His heart and He has titled the ensuing chapters of our lives. The outcome of His intention is the finishing line He intends that we reach. When we start with the future and work back to the present we get to understand the outline of our story and we can partner with the Holy Spirit to walk the path of that particular process. God uses our imagination to cultivate His intentions for us. We partner with

---

* For a more complete understanding of this revelatory truth look at *Living Your Truest Identity*, available at www.brilliantbookhouse.com

His intentionality and discover the faith, focus and favor that He willingly makes available.

If the outline of our story is already written, isn't it time that we understood it, stepped into it, and began partnering with God in its unfolding process?

Personal Notes

What scriptures and prophecies do you already possess?

Read through them; write down the key words and phrases that are outlined in the text. Are there any descriptive words about identity, promises or experiences? These all belong to you.

Use them to begin to outline in bullet point form the upgrades God has already authored.

Dream a little. Imagine yourself becoming that person and see what you are called to do in the Kingdom.

Write it down, follow the steps, start a new chapter.

Process always makes us rich

Imagine standing in 2013 and hearing God speak to you from 2023. He sees who you are there and relays that to you in your present. He sees it as a done deal and releases it to you as a "now" word. We hear it as a "future" word that needs to unfold its reality as we journey with God.

Future words give us an outcome that reshapes our story and changes our journey. Literally our current walk is upgraded and our relationship with God is redefined in line with His intention.

Once God has spoken He takes possession of our outcome and renames it destiny. His outlook on our identity becomes the ground of our expectation and favor in the present. Jesus takes our destiny in His hands and walks towards us in the present, interceding for us that we will achieve His objective (Hebrews 7:25).

Once God has spoken we take possession of the word and begin to outline our identity. Our outlook on His destiny for us becomes the image that we allow the Holy Spirit to cultivate into the likeness of Jesus. We take our identity in our hands and walk into the future partnering with the Holy Spirit on the way.

Somewhere on that journey identity meets destiny and we have an encounter with God that accelerates our development dramatically.

Process is the series of steps from identity initiated to outcome being released. It is the walk from who we are now to who we are becoming. All the obstacles on our journey are designed to establish our identity into destiny. The process is where we connect with the Lord and build the relationship that Jesus died to impart. Everything between prophecy spoken and fulfilled is designed to empower us to grow up in all things in Christ and learn to overcome through faith, focus and favor. It is this process that makes us rich in the life of the Spirit and the expectancy of the Kingdom.

In the ongoing development of our circumstances the process makes us rich as we focus on the outcome that God has decreed. When we have an agreed outcome we can do more than survive the process. We can learn to prosper from it. Process is about training in alignment with God. We exercise our faith in line with outcome promised, not the problem that is present. We work out our salvation in line with God's specific intention for us. We prepare the ground of our heart in faithfulness and obedience to God's chosen will. We practice the character required to fulfill our destiny. We use every situation to rehearse the identity that the Lord has revealed. We are being schooled by the Holy Spirit in the process of life. Enjoy the journey by allowing the richness of relationship to develop in the process you engage.

Personal Notes

What kind of person must you become to achieve the destiny God has proposed for you? That is the journey you must undertake in Christ.

Your perception of yourself: the way you think about your identity, and the language you develop for your journey must all be upgraded.

The real you is not stressed

Even a cursory look at Romans 6 tells us that our old nature is crucified with Christ and is therefore dead and buried. We are given permission to consider ourselves dead to sin and to only live as those who are alive to God, walking in the newness of life that He is creating in us, using our life situations.

We are permitted to think from a place of death not towards it. Death automatically means we are dead. This is indisputable in the natural world. It is also certainly the case in the realm of the Spirit. Therefore, crucifying the flesh is a consequence, not an action. We are dead in Christ. It is our pleasure and privilege to stay dead.

When we practice being alive to God, death is made more real and more permanent in our experience. We walk in newness of life by putting off the old man (Ephesians 4:20–24; Colossians 3:9–10) and putting on the new. We do not work on our old nature; we leave it in the grave. We work on our new nature in Jesus by establishing His righteousness internally using every adverse situation available to us. As we practice being alive to God we will be inspired and stimulated by His nature, not our old habits.

We are dead in Christ, therefore God does not see what is wrong with us because He nailed all those things to the Cross (Colossians 2:14) and has no desire to resurrect them. He does not see what is wrong with us; He only sees what is currently missing from our experience of Christ. He is deeply committed to that ongoing experience by the power of the indwelling Spirit. He is focused on our new nature in Jesus. That means when He puts His finger on a part of our life that is not fully functioning in relationship with Him, He is actually pointing to the site of our next upgrade in Christ. God has no bad thought toward us, only a desire to see us conform to the image of Jesus!

Our new nature, with its new voice, must take control over the old self and the stress it provokes. The presence of Jesus as the Prince of Peace must war on all anxiety, fear and intimidation. Jesus is the antidote to all negativity. The fruit of the Spirit (Galatians 5:22–23) makes joyful opposition to all bad habits.

Our new nature, conforming to the image of Jesus creates a new realm within that overcomes the pressures of the external world. Stress is a by-product of a life not focused on Christ within. The Prince of Peace must take up residence. It is the work of the Spirit to take what belongs to Jesus and makes it real to us (John 16:15). As we partner with that process we learn to face life in all the character and attributes of Jesus.

Personal Notes

What would it be like for you to wage war on anxiety and fear using peace as a weapon?

How do you plan to stay dead while walking in newness of life?

What is missing from your current experience of Jesus?

Make a list and ask the Father which one He is upgrading first. Practice what He shows you and enjoy becoming more of who He is for you!

Identity accelerates the impossible

It's impossible! It can't be done! How often does our lack of imagination or faith cause us to make the impossible become our truth of convenience? We take the line of least resistance when we give up without really trying. Thus the impossible becomes merely the untried.

When we use logic instead of faith the impossible becomes our language of defeat. We forget that we are in Christ and defect to the mindset of man rather than the perspective of God.

When we say that something is "out of the question" we deny ourselves the relational dialogue that could prove the opposite. When we mark something as unachievable we forget that Christ in us (Colossians 1:27) is the reality of God's ability to produce after His kind. We make unattainable what is beyond our ability to see in the natural realm. We become earthbound in our focus when we disconnect from the Kingdom where all things are a possibility.

What is impossible for man is possible with God. In Christ we are encouraged to explore a life beyond a logical thought process. "God is able to do exceedingly, abundantly beyond all that we could ask or even think, according to the power that works in us" (Ephesians 3:20). What is beyond thinking? Surely that would be imagination and dreaming? All the great technological breakthroughs in the earth began with a dream breaking through the logical, impossible barrier of underachievement.

Our language in the Kingdom is derived from our relationship with God's nature. "I can do all things through Christ, who strengthens me" (Philippians 4:13). God allows in His wisdom what He could easily prevent by His power. If He allows an impossibility to connect with us, it is because He desires to unite us with the terms of His own capacity to create. The impossible only signals where our ability stops and His continue. In that place of tension He reinforces our trust and enhances our desire to see a miracle.

"All things are possible, only believe" (Mark 9:23). The language of all relationship is the vocabulary of trust. We express our confidence in a variety of ways. God uses our life situations to enhance the terminology of the Kingdom in our worldly circumstances.

It is vital then that we do not allow impossibilities to weaken our resolve to pursue astonishment. Amazement occurs when the natural laws of man are overturned by the sovereignty of God. When God moves in His possibilities, our weakness receives strength. What would debilitate us is instead renewed, and we are encouraged to press into the bigness of God.

Surely, anyone can trust God for the ordinary. *Extraordinary* people believe for the impossible. It's the perspective of the Kingdom. The impossible enlarges our inner world with God's greatness. It's worth the risk to discover that higher majesty.

Personal Notes

What seemingly impossible thing are you facing at this current moment? What do you imagine the Lord is connecting you to in His purpose?

What is the expression of trust that you need to make in line with God's sovereignty? What new language is now possible?

What new questions should you be asking? This is the place of your enlargement. What is growing in your spirit?

What is God replacing in you?

Someone very close to me wrote me a letter regarding the intimidation they were experiencing in a particular situation. Advice was being sought on how to deal with this debilitating negative emotion.

In the Kingdom that we inhabit, all negativity has been laid on Jesus. He bore it in His own body so that we could be free. He was separated from the Father so we could always be in relationship. Every negative thought and emotion persecuted Jesus so that He cried out, "My Father, why have you forsaken me?" Jesus, in the agony of separation asked the "why" question.

This question is never answered on earth. It is a victim question. It's an invalid question that makes us an invalid in our circumstances. The Good News is that Jesus did not just die for us, He died *as* us! He took all our afflictions, mental, emotional, physical and spiritual upon Himself.

Our old nature is dead and intimidation with it. That curse is broken by sacrifice. Our new nature is learning to abide in our true identity in Jesus. We merely have a default habit that causes us to repeat a defeat rather than upgrade to a new behavior.

In the Kingdom we inhabit there are no negatives, only positives yet to be explored and appropriated. God is in the business of putting things into place that belong to His identity so that we can become like Him.

What if we are not intimidated? What if the real issue is that we have not fully grasped the identity that is in us in Christ? The words the Lord speaks to us by revelation of scripture or insights of prophecy are designed to elevate our perception of what it means to be Christlike in our thinking and perception. In Christ we never have to fight a negative because He has already beaten it!

We never deal with a negative thought in the way it attacks us. The enemy would seek to use that thought to occupy our attention and bring us low. In Christ we get to take that thought captive and replace it with a better one. This is what we call renewing of the mind. Our mind is not renewed by battling against a negative thought. It can only be redeemed by receiving the mind of Christ and thinking the way that He would, now that He is in our life circumstances.

We have the mind of Christ. So the issue becomes: what is He replacing in us that allows us to overcome a negative? What if intimidation is being upgraded to courage so that we are astonished at the power of the one, with the ONE!

Jesus makes all things new so that we walk in newness of life. We cannot be captured by an old habit when we have a new nature. Abiding in Christ means that we are only engaged with putting on the new man. This identity is renewed in the knowledge of Christ. Our old man is dead (Romans 6:11); we are putting away the old, not trying to fix it (Ephesians 4:20–24; Colossians 3:9–10).

Whatever is the opposite of intimidation (which is only a form of bullying) is actually what the Holy Spirit is establishing in us. The life of Christ will always move in the opposite Spirit to the world, the flesh and the devil. When reviled, we bless; we love our enemies; we practice joy in adversity. In Christ we have the privilege of turning every negative into its opposite, so that we can reveal the nature of God. Every time we feel intimidated in our soul we can rejoice in our spirit man because we know we can partner with God in upgrading who we are in Him.* That's really purposeful!

We are learning to turn intimidation to our advantage. That is what favor empowers us to do. We turn the tables on the enemy so we can profit from the attack. This is our heritage in the Lord.

---

* For a more full description of the difference between soul and spirit, look at the printed journal or eBook entitled *Towards a Powerful Inner Life*.

Personal Notes

This is your opportunity to learn to move in the opposite spirit. Do not confront the negative directly. Find the opposite thought and cultivate the anointing that goes with it.

Record the negative thought in your journal. Then, write down the opposite thought that comes from the mind of Christ.

What is the difference? What changes in you as you embrace the thoughts of Heaven? What is the difference in your perception, thinking and language? What actions are now possible?

Keep a reckoning in your journal.

Personal Notes

11

God always hides in plain sight!

Personal Notes

The Holy Spirit is teaching us how to see the Lord in everyday circumstances. It is so simple even a child can see the Kingdom at work all around us.

Be wholehearted in your love of God and your capacity to see Him will grow accordingly. Children have a sense of wonder that governs their daily lives. In that creative mindset they get to envision every situation in a way that pleases them.

What is wrong with that? God is in you, with you, for you.

Imagine that and you will see Him. Simple really.

Being stretched is the key to growth

This one thing I do, forgetting what lies behind I reach out to what is before me and press onto the prize of the high call of God in Christ (Philippians 3:13–14).

Allowing ourselves to reach out in the Spirit to pursue fullness and abundance will cause us to be stretched beyond our current limitations. This creates an inner space that ultimately will be filled with the goodness of God.

The Father works from the initial to the eventual. Initially His promises open us up to all His possibilities of favor and expectation. We reach out for the prize and are struck by the violence of the circumstance. Deliverance does not come to our order but by God's consent. We are pressed out of shape, beyond our measure to receive, and outside of our comfort zone.

The inaugural word of God that got us to move forward seems not to produce anything as it has in former times. Believe and you shall receive is one order of Kingdom business. Learning obedience and faithfulness in the face of nothing changing is another form of growth and development.

Sometimes we inherit eventually. The promise seems imminent but the fruit appears later looking like a crown rather than a prize. The key to this conundrum is sensitivity to the Holy Spirit. We must not assume that our past lesson in the area of trust is being repeated. The exercise of our faith may be different. The apparatus in a gym is designed to work different parts of the body. So it is with life lessons in faith, trust and believing.

When upgrading us God takes us beyond our own ability to generate anything from our past experience. This is a new lesson. We move into a place of believing and expectation and are then stretched out on the rack of nothing happening.

Our capacity to hold onto Heaven whilst the earth seems to be spinning out of control puts pressure on our trust. Sometimes breakthrough occurs when we do not snap back to a default position.

12

At other times our trust is the prize that God seeks to bestow. In matters of trust development, the words 'though' and 'yet' are the prime tools of our growth and eventual advance. "Though He slay me, yet will I trust in Him", spoken by Job in very stretching, relationship defining circumstances (Job 13:15).

Habakkuk 3:17–19: "Though the fig tree should not blossom and there be no fruit on the vines, though the yield of the olive should fail and the fields produce no food, though the flock should be cut off from the fold and there be no cattle in the stalls, yet I will exult in the LORD, I will rejoice in the God of my salvation. The Lord GOD is my strength; and He has made my feet like hinds' feet, and makes me walk on my high places. For the choir director, on my stringed instruments."

"Though and yet," define our evolution in the realm of trust and faithfulness.

The word "though" means: in spite of events. The word "yet" means: because of who God really is, we will pursue Him personally, not the outcome that He can generate. Relationship with Him is worth more than the resolution of our problems.

Here's the thing: sometimes we receive under pressure and we are elated. Other times our lesson was not about receiving but simply about trusting and being stretched beyond measure in our faithfulness.

In the goodness of God if we do not receive initially we will eventually because God is faithful to us. He will always honor our trust.

Every believer needs stretch marks. They define the quality of our obedience and our willingness to reach out to what the Father is putting in front of us. In this place of development there can be no disappointment only the sure and certain knowledge that all promises eventually are fulfilled.

Always ask the Lord if a lesson is being repeated. Sometimes the outcome that God requires is not the resolution of a difficulty but the cultivation of a specific aspect of His nature.

There will never be a conference on patience. No one would show up and speakers would decline to attend. Patience cannot be acquired in a weekend. Neither can faithfulness or trust.

When you are being stretched beyond your measure it is always about your being made Christlike. Grit your teeth and worship. Give thanks as long as you are able. There is no pass mark. He may not tell you what pleased Him about your conduct and He will not judge your attainment.

Eventually, you will know what has become different for you. Usually an increase of presence, love, peace or joy. Perhaps a greater capacity to endure and persist.

Stay true, that's the main thing. Think about whatever seems good to you in the context of this lesson. Love the learning.

13

Presence is always tangible

Presence is always real whether we are feeling His company or believing that His Spirit is in attendance. In faith we receive Him because of the truth of His word; "I will never leave you nor forsake you. I am with you always, even until the end of the world" (Hebrews 13:5, Matthew 28:20). Faith makes God manifest. He said He would never leave us therefore He is here! Faith does not need emotions but is complemented by them. What we believe for is eventually made real in solid form. God loves to materialize and make His presence felt in our heart.

At the dedication of Solomon's temple (1 Kings 8:11), God came and filled the place and no one could stay on their feet. Tangible presence affects us physically, mentally, emotionally and spiritually. God is real and that reality can overwhelm us on any given day. Moses saw a burning bush and heard the voice coming out of it (Exodus 3:2–4). Elisha saw horses and chariots of fire (2 Kings 6:17). Paul was knocked off his horse and blinded for several days by the brilliant light that surrounded him (Acts 9:3–9). The disciples on the road to Emmaus felt their hearts burn within them when Jesus was present but hidden (Luke 24:13–32).

The fruit of the Spirit (Galatians 5:22–23) interacts with our emotions as we engage with love, joy and peace and the rest.

God's presence goes with us and we experience His rest (Exodus 33:14). Peace interrupts our circumstances. All anxiety and fear is suspended by presence. We live in the stillness of majesty and revel in the quietness of His Spirit.

Every situation has something tangible to release in either faith or feelings. Both these extremes bring us to the exact same place in terms of manifestation. It is quite simply door A or door B into the Throne Room.

There is only one voice to be heard from Heaven. It can be audible, loud enough to be heard physically; or discernible, perceived by faith in the stillness of our spirit. I love both and have been governed by each extreme. That voice has the wonderful capacity to make us feel good about ourselves. His presence makes us glad. There is joy (pleasure, delight and laughter) forevermore.

It is vital to enter His presence. When was your last tangible encounter with God physically and emotionally? Ask and keep on asking for a fresh impartation into your feelings.

When was the last time you believed His presence was with you regardless of feelings? It is wonderful to trust the word of the Lord, and to expect His presence because He is truthful. Faith is not better than feelings, just different. God has given all things richly to enjoy (1 Timothy 6:17). To be wholesome requires both ends of a paradox to be enjoyed enthusiastically. Faith and feelings make us normal, fruitful, powerful and deeply relational.

14

Refreshing in a constant

The promise of God is that we will have internal rivers of water flowing into everlasting life (John 7:38). The goal and blessing of our life is that we live in the accords of Heaven. On earth as it is in Heaven was the prayer of Jesus (Matthew 6:10). Our spirituality and what we can expect from the sovereign Lord is defined by such statements.

We take our cues from Heaven not the world around us. We are in the world but not of it (1 Corinthians 1:20–31). The world has nothing to teach us about the Kingdom that orchestrates our lives. As citizens of Heaven on earth we live in the attitudes and grand designs of an altogether different realm. This is a domain that is undefeated, contains no negatives and is uniquely powerful in all aspects of the Christ life. Crucially it is a Kingdom that does not incorporate dryness in any form.

In Christ we are always more subject to refreshing than dehydration. Heaven has never been arid, thirsty or parched. The very nature of the Christ life is overflowing with renewal and refreshing, life giving water. Revival is concerned not with an evangelistic event but a company of people living in the fullness of the river of God (Ezekiel 47:9). Everything lives where the river flows. We live lives of fullness, abundance, renewal and restoration. We stay fresh, invigorated and revived. We know how to abide in the active, energetic, unwearied presence of God.

The physical land around us may be arid and dry but we have water in the wilderness (Psalm 107:35).

Our spirit remains in the presence of God and overcomes the dryness of our soul. We have water in the desert, which is a euphemism for ongoing wealth and abundance of life, and riches. To live at an oasis in the desert is the very symbol of power. Everyone must come to those who have access to life-giving water. Everything lives where the river flows.

We will never be thirsty again if Christ is the very source of our life. Never means under no circumstances are we vulnerable to the dryness. There are no occasions where the well runs dry as we abide in the fullness of Jesus. In Christ we can never make allowances for failure or defeat. Instead we are encouraged to a fullness of expectation. There is a favor upon us that belongs to His majesty. Heaven adores Jesus and gladly pours out refreshing on all those living life in His name. We are refreshed forever by presence.

Personal Notes

In Christ you are destined to overflow in even the driest places. Read this prophetic word aloud into your circumstances:

> This is a place of My outpouring in your life. It is a place of Renewal and Refreshing. I have given you My Spirit. Receive Him. Be filled to overflowing. Be invigorated! Be restored! Be refreshed! Be renewed. Be healed. This is the place of health to your body. You shall experience My body becoming yours.
>
> My word shall heal you in this place. My word shall be your health in this place. I rule over your body with My own. My fullness is healing you. My energy is your stamina. My zeal is your passion says the Lord of Hosts.
>
> You are restored to First Love. You are a worshiper. Enter your place of thanksgiving, rejoicing and praise. Become invigorated in worship. I am giving you mental, physical, emotional and spiritual restoration through the power of rejoicing.
>
> The joy of your God is your strength. ENCOUNTER MY MAJESTY. The water level is rising. The water level is rising. The water level is rising. The water level is rising. The water level is rising. The water level is rising. Receive your upgrade. Receive your increase. Abide in both. Be renewed and refreshed. Stay here until I am satisfied with your renewal and fullness.

What is stirring in your heart?

What refreshing is available to you at this time?

What must change in you to ensure that you are always refreshed?

15

Impossibility thinking

People always want to talk about the odds *against* something happening. They will have the opinion that declares something is 90% improbable. The mind of Christ declares that a 10% chance of success is good enough to launch something as an idea, "what is impossible with man is possible with God" (Luke 18:27).

As we continue with God the odds *for* something begin to increase. The foundation of God's nature is always our starting point for any enterprise. When we know Him properly, we behold His majesty. When we know that we are His Beloved, we bask in His favor. When we know the power of the one with the ONE, then it is our privilege to trust Him.

We never figure the odds against, only the odds for something to occur. Our lives in Christ have more trust, more faith and more fun attached than we often realize. It is sensible to count the cost before commencing an enterprise. However, we do so in order to calculate what God needs to be for us in the endeavor. What does need to happen to bring an idea to fruition? What are the time frames and priorities? The answers to those questions tell us how to come before God in prayer.

There is too much passion in the Holy Spirit for us ever to be stuck in a negative place. Passion counts the cost differently. We plan something based upon what God is doing in us and through us. We have to factor in the call of God upon us, and the prophecies and inheritance words of scripture that belong to us. All the intentions of God are part of our resources for the project.

Dreams are not fulfilled by the sensible. True passion loves the impossible. It is energized by it. Passion does not partner with conventional thinking. Passion is like water. It seeps into the space surrounding an obstacle. It maneuvers around objects and barriers. It finds a way through. Passion is resourceful. Trust always partners with passion to develop the faith to overcome.

God never lies and He can only do what is right. Trust is confidence in the very words of God. Passion is a strong delight in the nature of God that governs our fellowship with Him.

When combined, they position us to believe the intentions of God in the matter at hand. Together, they form the "stance" in our circumstance.

All projects come to a fork in the road. In one direction is a way that seems right. Logic and reason would take us down that road. It's the road where we determine what is possible through the resources we can generate. By that thinking maybe ten people would have had a snack with the five loaves and two fish; rather than the 5,000 who were full with twelve baskets of food remaining!

The other way is the road of intuition that leads to creative thinking. Wisdom is the knowledge of how God perceives, thinks, speaks, and likes to do something. Let passion choose the direction. Allow your renewed mind to serve God in faith. When met by an obstacle we must use it to increase the size of the dream.

God places the obstacles in front of us. The obstruction is not a stumbling block. Every hindrance is a benefit instead. The size of the difficulty determines the provision we need to negotiate it. That is a cause for excitement! God allows in His wisdom what He could easily prevent by His power. He is Lord over all things therefore every obstacle belongs to Him. He places the barrier in front of us to teach us about His advancement.

If an obstruction blocks our vision then we must receive elevation in the Spirit to see beyond it and move forward. Everything works for good! A restriction encourages us to see what God wants to open. A limitation teaches us that an upgrade in our resources is currently available. If we are in Christ then so are all our circumstances. If we can never be separated from the love of God (Romans 8:35–39) then our problems can never be separated from the faith that God has for our life.

Personal Notes

If you are to overcome the obstacle, what needs to happen in your heart? How must your thinking change to reflect the mind of Christ? What new strategies will the Holy Spirit turn into actions? What will be your new "stance" before God in your circumstance? What are the odds for you in the plan and purpose of God?

Focus provides high definition

It should not matter how much the enemy spins us around in life situations. Christ is the center of who we are, which means we have a fixed point to which we always return. The Holy Spirit will always make Jesus our focal point for response. In Christ, the enemy is never allowed to determine our focus. We use the enemy to define the current experience of majesty that God wants to bestow upon us.

When we define a circumstance we are stating the meaning that it holds for us in our relationship with God's majesty. Many years ago the Father asked this author a question. "Graham, what would it take for you to believe that I AM unceasingly magnificent toward you?" We are still having an ongoing dialogue about this issue and the lifestyle it provokes. We define our lives by the plans, purpose and intentions of God. All our circumstances are a part of His clarity towards us. They call us up to a higher place of significance in Christ. Problems show us God's predetermined purpose. Problems are designed to make our promises more visible. Every problem is therefore part of an upgraded experience that God has set aside for us in the current situation.

The Holy Spirit is the personification of focus. He takes everything that belongs to Jesus and reveals it to us in life. He specifies what belongs to us *because* of the circumstance. He describes to us how we should come before God and how we should stand against the enemy. He is our HELPER in all things. We are never alone, ever! As we learn what we need to move forward, we also learn who we are becoming now in Christ. Every life situation carries an upgrade in who Christ is for us and who we are becoming in Him. We are literally learning how to grow up in all things in Christ. He is becoming an increasingly stronger part of our fullness. The fullness of Christ provides the conduct class where we develop abundance in our thoughts and actions. When the Holy Spirit defines our circumstances He also designates what belongs to us in the situation. When He designates we learn what to pray for in the problem. "We have not because we ask not" (James 4:2).

Usually, we have not because we did not hear the Holy Spirit telling us what He is providing.

When the Holy Spirit defines our circumstances then we must work on our own definitions in line with His intention. This is our first response. We now state the meaning of the situation back to Him. Our language is: "this is what God is doing for me, in me, and through me, using this situation." We describe the purpose of God and our own actions in response. Then we use those thoughts in our rejoicing, thanksgiving and worship. This creates a huge alignment between our hearts and the Holy Spirit and eliminates the space where doubt would normally be lurking.

Everything about the Christ life is connected to height. We are seated with Christ in Heavenly Places (Ephesians 2:5–6). We learn to set our mind on things above, not on things on the earth (Colossians 3:1–3).

In Christ we have elevated status, permission to overcome and legal authority over the enemy.* We are raised up in Christ to occupy a place far above all that would seek to bring us down. This involves a mindset, an approach to majesty and a language that is aligned to ascendency as a lifestyle.

The activities of the enemy therefore can only concentrate our focus on the sovereignty of Jesus. Joshua and Caleb understood this point perfectly when they declared their own definition of the conquest of Canaan to the people of Israel (Numbers 14:6–9). "If the Lord is pleased with us, then He will bring us into this land and give it to us; a land which flows with milk and honey. Only do not rebel against the Lord; and do not fear the people of the land, for they shall be our prey. Their protection has been removed from them, and the Lord is with us; do not fear them."

That is a definition based upon the designation of God! Sadly, most of their generation never aligned themselves with that definition and perished in their poverty mindset. In Christ we never start with a deficit. We begin with His fullness and we align ourselves with the current expression of that in our present position.

---

* For much more on this, listen to the CD set *Living Your Truest Identity*

Personal Notes

The Holy Spirit is challenging us to rethink our assumptions. What does focus mean to you? How will you define current circumstances in line with who God is for you?

Take some time to hear the Spirit define what God is doing. Create your response and the "stance" you will make in alignment with God's intention.

You have some writing to do!

Personal Notes

17

There is always enough Light

The point of darkness is to release the light. The light shines in the darkness, and the darkness did not comprehend it (John 1:5). The darkness cannot stop something it cannot understand. It cannot penetrate something that is unfathomable. The enemy is destined to misunderstand God's ultimate purpose. If he had known the purpose of Christ in redemption, he would have chopped down every tree in Israel! His own darkness is so pervasive he will continually misinterpret events and miss the point of what God is doing.

He seeks to make us vulnerable to that which he is subject; misapprehension. This is the capacity to interpret events from a lower order of being. Since the fall from Heaven he is out of the loop regarding ultimate purpose. The enemy wants to develop that same blindness in us so that we are in the dark about the purposes of God towards us. Doubt, mistrust, fear, anxiety, tension and apprehension are all constructs of being in the dark rather than living in the Shadow of the Almighty (Psalm 91:1).

Jesus came saying: "I AM the Light of the world; he who follows Me will not walk in darkness, but will have the Light of Life" (John 8:12). Light is essential to this life in the Spirit. We are to walk as children who stay in the light (Ephesians 5:8). We fight the darkness best by remaining in the light. We fight only on God's terms. We are in Christ who is our light and life. His light brings revelation, which gives us the ability to see in the dark. Revelation is concerned with God's disclosure and our admission that it is true. Insight prevails regardless of circumstances. Revelation is often a shock to our system and an absolute bombshell to the enemy. True light exposes that which does not originate in Christ. When revelation occurs we must step into the light it brings and walk into newness of life. The darkness that has clung to us must be expelled along with all the negativity that it produced.

God's word functions as a lamp to our feet and a light to our path (Psalm 119:105). There is a present/future aspect to walking in the light. Sometimes God illuminates only the space around our feet because He is teaching us to walk step by step with Him, in the here and now. He will not bow to our need to know details regarding how it will work out in the future. We learn trust on a day-to-day basis.

At other times His word is a light to the path ahead of us and we step into a broader place of illumination and intention that allows us to look further in front of our present placement. When God illuminates the future He is reorienting our present into a larger understanding and experience of His purposes for us. He needs us to become more familiar with our destiny so He upgrades our current identity in line with His future intention. We must have time to acclimate to a higher position and become accustomed to the desires of God for us in this new space.

Reorientation is a crucial part of our development where we make adjustments in alignment with intention. Our sense of direction is augmented and our new location in the Spirit impacts upon our current situation. We rise up as we grow up.

Wisdom excels folly as light excels darkness (Ecclesiastes 2:13). As we walk in the light our capacity to exceed is greater than the ability of darkness to prevent. We learn how to prevail against any opposition. Abundance increases when resistance is present. When the enemy contends we can abound. It is not enough for the people of God to survive in circumstances. We must triumph! We can learn the art of conquest with success. We cannot just engage in defensive warfare. We must overcome to the point where the enemy becomes wary of fighting against us. We are more than conquerors (Romans 8:37) when he fails to show up for the fight. We out-rival our chief rival.

We dare not conceive of life outside the splendor of Christ. The Light of His majesty shines through us in all earthly situations. This is what it means to walk in newness of life.

Personal Notes

Can you identify your current darkness where anxiety, doubt and fear have penetrated? What light have you received in recent times, either by prophecy or personal revelation? Have your circumstances adjusted to this higher level of being? Are you learning to walk step by step in the light? If so, it is your relationship in trust, rejoicing and being God conscious that is being upgraded.

If you are seeing things further ahead then you are learning more about your destiny. Your identity needs to come into greater alignment with God's increased purpose.

Take time to rethink who you are in the Light of God.

Knowing your "stance" in the circumstance

18

"One who doubts is like the surf of the sea, driven and tossed by the wind. For that man ought not expect that he will receive anything from the Lord, being a double minded man, unstable in all his ways" (James 1:6–8).

When we doubt we are aiding the enemy in his desire to render us ineffective. We are providing key support in our own demise. The instability that doubt provides spreads from one initial area to cover others making us unstable in all. Surrender can become exponential.

If we are going to yield, it must be to the passion and loving-kindness of God. We make ourselves gladly vulnerable to the majesty of Jesus. Doubt debilitates but focus provides stamina, power and influence from the Lord. Focus enables us to plan ahead and strategize at the level that the Lord wishes to release into our lives.

Life is primarily determined by the level on which we are engaging the Holy Spirit, and what we are hearing and seeing in God's heart. When we are not partaking of fellowship at the appropriate level then we determine life through the events around us and how we perceive them. We are the surf subject to the wind of circumstance. We know when our level needs to be expanded when we begin to lose focus in our circumstances. Focus is tangible perception and follows the path of our worship and intimacy. We engage more easily with what we adore. When the Lord sets our current level, His presence increases no matter the events of life. Focus turns all things to our advantage. We are exhilarated, not overwhelmed, by situations. We find the good that God wills and we abide in that place. We look for majesty, not rescue.

When we stop trusting we must upgrade focus so that we can ask in line with God's favor. It is time for elevation. We need to gain more height in our pursuit of relationship with God. Height increases perspective! Elevation is connected to our promotion and advance. It gives us prominence by increasing our stature in the Kingdom. It intensifies our permission and increases faith. Our language changes as we enter a new level.

Elevation is a process of upgrading focus. To heighten means our language and mindset is raised to see God differently. To elevate is to advance to a higher level and position. Our state changes both internally and otherwise. To exalt is to be raised very high in rank, character, mindset and authority. To be enhanced in our relationship with God means that we are attracted to Jesus at a new level of desire, delight and passion.

Spiritual focus is the critical focal point of concentration between the Father, us and our situation. We want His perspective, thinking and language. We take those on board and are fully adjusted in our relationship to a new place of fellowship. Paul exemplifies that in His statement in 2 Timothy 1:12. "I know whom I have believed and I am convinced that He is able to guard what I have entrusted to Him until that day." That is a stance. He has taken a position in his circumstances that allows no provision for doubt or dismay. I know and I am fully persuaded. Focus makes us categorical.

Focus provides us with a converging point in worship and faith. It enables thanksgiving and uses the key of joy to rejoice in all things. In focus we count all things as joy because we are governed by a perspective that elevates our mindset in alignment with what God is thinking.

As we adjust our focus we are positioned properly to take full advantage of all that is happening. We have a new place to stand before God, men and the enemy. We have a renewed "stance" in our circumstance.

Personal Notes

It is time for you to think about your upward call. What level are you on now? Where is the Lord taking you next? Examine your personal words from God, how is He describing you?

What is holding you back on this level? It is time to learn to adapt yourself to the level where you can overcome.

19

It's Time!

Now is the accepted time. Today is the day. We are learning to be present to the moment in Christ. This ensures that we are up to date with regard to His current purpose.

Paul's statement of focus was: "this one thing I do. Forgetting what lies behind and reaching forward to what lies ahead. I press on towards the goal for the prize of the upward call of God in Christ Jesus" (Philippians 3:14–15). Paul's "one thing" is an objective with three purposes! This is the primary point of focus. It increases our intention. It covers every eventuality within the objective. Focus opens us up to the process we need to take to realize the goal that the Father wants us to achieve.

An upgrade has three stages. Firstly, we must move on from where we have been. Closure is a vital part of advancement. In Christ we are present/future and not present/past. Focus enables us to know our distractions and move beyond them. Focus produces priorities. We move from the inner core of presence to the outer place where we engage with the world around us. Failure to establish the inner core of relationship means that we are overwhelmed by external events rather than by the nature of God within in Christ. In Him we live and move and have our being. Great focus always comes from great presence.

When we reach out to what God is doing in front of us, it is our focus that creates energy. All focus is derived from the passion of the Holy Spirit for Jesus (John 16:7–15), and His pleasure in declaring and demonstrating Christ within. Revelation changes our focus and increases power. What we focus on gives us power to pursue. We zoom in on the real picture.

As we take hold of what we are seeing in regard to our upgrade we have to learn to press into Christ in our advancement. We face two battles over everything. One battle to take ground and another to hold that new territory. It is one battle to get free and another to stay free. Many people win the first but lose the second. All breakthroughs and upgrades must be established in our lifestyle. The first battle is where we have an encounter with God and something tangible occurs that creates new momentum. After this comes a series of situations designed to take that breakthrough into all our life situations by on ongoing experience. There is no breakthrough without follow-through. If we do not turn encounter into an ongoing experience then we have met God but not been transformed by Him. We will default back to our previous pattern of behavior when the pressure is on us.

When we recognize our time we must cooperate with the Holy Spirit to redeem the time by taking advantage of God's presence, now! Time is a valuable commodity. Foolish people waste time. Good people find time. Great people make time for the realities of God. Redeeming time is crucial. Time is the currency of our lives, not money. Our prophecies and promises are the medium of exchange in the Kingdom. Favor is the legal tender that they generate.

When we take time to rethink the purpose of God toward us, we can step into a new, more powerful place of beholding and becoming.

Regardless of circumstances, this is your time to have a fresh encounter with God. When positioning yourself for an encounter you must also know that you need to set aside several weeks to develop the encounter into a life experience. What is the encounter that God wants to give you? What are the problems and situations that need to be transformed into new experiences in Christ?

Sit quietly and ask the Lord to speak to you about encounter and experiences. One leads to the others. The follow-through only occurs when we know what God wants to transform in our life situations.

Disappointment occurs when our experience of the truth is much smaller than our knowledge of it.

20

When God shows you something, the knowledge of it must translate into experiences that transform your life.

To be ankle deep in blessing is the lowest form of spiritual expression. Read Ezekiel 47:3–5. There are four measures of encounter and growth. You must move beyond the initial encounter with the Savior to an ongoing experience of the Lordship of Christ that covers all our life demands and pressures.

When you know a lot but your experience is minimal, you are merely religious with an earthbound spirituality that cannot empower you to reach the heights of what Jesus wants to be for you.

God is measuring you for more than a blessing. He is measuring you for a transformation. Time to take stock!

21

Do not battle fear. Embrace love!

When we receive the Lord Jesus at salvation we inherit everything that He is and we learn progressively how to walk in His fullness. The work of the Holy Spirit is to empower us to be firmly rooted and comprehensively built up in Him. All our circumstances are designed to enable us to be established in our faith and to be overflowing with gratitude.

As we remain in His fullness we learn how to stay vulnerable to His fullness and are therefore not to be subject to the world around us and its principles and practices. There is a completion in Christ so powerful that it empowers us to move in His authority and rule in all life situations.

All that was formerly against us has been summarily dealt with by the Cross of Jesus. All the debts and decrees against us; every hostile act upon our person have been removed from us by His sacrifice. We are dead to it and we have the gravestone to prove it. We are raised up to walk in newness of life. Nothing from the past can affect us unless we allow it (Colossians 2:6–14, my paraphrase).

Sin, with all its consequences and effects, has been powerfully removed. We are learning only about the fullness of Christ in His heavenly form. He came to earth as the Son of Man to live a sinless life and be our sacrifice. He now lives in us as the victorious and glorious Son of God to commission us to walk in His grace and favor. There are no negatives in Him. All curses are broken. He is our ancestral line. We inherit His fullness and are no longer subject to a past earthly heritage. All negativity has been displaced by His death on our behalf. We are becoming ever more aware of our freedoms. Our starting place for life in the death of Jesus and all that He provides in Himself.

We never fight a negative; we simply look beyond it and move into our freedom. We do not battle fear, we embrace the love that belongs to us in Christ. Our favor in Christ allows us to find the opposite of any negative and embrace that as our attitude, mindset and lifestyle. In every situation of life it is our pleasure and privilege to incorporate all that Jesus is, into all that we are not. He is our medium of exchange. In Christ, the Father replaces old with new. There is no requirement for us to work on the old but simply to put it away and put on the new person we are in Jesus. When we see any believer living in fear we know that the problem is not the negative lifestyle. That has been dealt with at the Cross. The real problem is that they are trying to overcome fear when really they need to be experiencing perfect love in Christ (1 John 4:18).

Have fun moving in the opposite spirit! We are learning to live as though a negative cannot be part of our life experience. The nature of God has swallowed up every form of death. Life in Christ has radiance so bright that all the dark shadows of negativity become sunspots of brilliance. Whatever God is, He is relentlessly. The Holy Spirit is relentless in making Jesus real to us in every single circumstance of life. Our ministry is to learn the beauty of exchange, firstly for ourselves, then to apply those truths relentlessly to others so that they can be set free.

Personal Notes

Never resist love. Allow the love of God to persist against all fear until it fully departs, never to return.

We persist through becoming steadfast in love. We relentlessly, joyfully pursue freedom as our right in the fullness of Christ. The Holy Spirit is resolute and joyfully determined to demonstrate what the fullness of Christ means in every situation.

We are being challenged by loving-kindness, goodness, freedom and favor in all our life issues. We never allow any negative to remain unchecked.

We are the Beloved of God in Christ. Life is to be enjoyed on that basis. List every negative against you. What is the opposite? Make a second list of opposites and destroy the first list. You now have a record of all that God is relentlessly doing in your life. Enjoy this process; it will turn you into another person.*

---

* For a full teaching on this issue, look up *Turning Passivity into Prophecy* at www.brilliantbookhouse.com

Fascination beats intimidation

The goal of all the working of the Holy Spirit is to make us like Jesus in everything. A major part of our experience with Him is that we become astonished at our new man in Christ. We are a new creation, all the old things are passed away, everything has become new and all things are of God, from God. (2 Corinthians 5:17–18)

One of the most enjoyable facets of this radiant life is that we should never be intimidated by our circumstances because we are too busy being fascinated by Jesus!

Nothing makes us fearful, timid or discouraged. Our gladness can never be subdued. We have an innate cheerfulness that comes from knowing that Jesus has already overcome.

In this life we are preoccupied with who Jesus is for us in every situation. We joyfully depend upon the brilliant Holy Spirit who is a genius at life in Christ. We exemplify the Good News. The rhythm of our life is solely concerned with our hearts and minds becoming captivated by Jesus. In every situation we are attracted to His fullness, and held by it until we have an experience that empowers us into renewal. We are gripped in our attention, delighted, enthralled and overpowered by all that Jesus is for us. Astonishment at Jesus is the key to being overwhelmed by the goodness of God. We overcome evil with good. Our privilege is to know only Jesus as the answer to all things.

Astonishment is a way of life for us.

Personal Notes

We are practicing a way of being astonished. The enemy cannot penetrate a clear sense of wonder. When he fell from Heaven he lost everything, and can now be defeated by anyone who lives in Heaven's atmosphere. Astonishment is the atmosphere of Heaven and the only environment that makes sense for us on earth.[*]

---

[*] For a more full understanding of this subject read *Living in Dependency and Wonder* available on www.brilliantbookhouse.com

When God grants you something, He expects you to take Him for granted!

In life we are always being challenged to want more of God. Heaven desires to release its resources to us. We must pray in line with God's purposes not our problems. We are often undone by our language. We pray like a widow when we should pray like a bride. We ask God to open a window in Heaven and pour out a blessing. This sounds spiritual until we understand that Jesus is the door that has been open in Heaven for 2,000 years. He ever lives to intercede for us (Hebrews 7:25) that we will comprehend who we really are and what is truly available to us.

Jesus quoted Isaiah 61 as His inheritance word so that people would have no doubt about what His ministry entailed. "The Spirit of the Lord is upon Me because He has anointed me to preach good tidings to the poor; He has sent Me to heal the brokenhearted, to proclaim liberty to the captives, and the opening of the prison to those who are bound. (Isaiah 61:1)

He came to grant those who mourn in Zion, giving them a garland instead of ashes; the oil of gladness instead of mourning, the mantle of praise instead of a spirit of fainting. So they will be called oaks of righteousness, the planting of the LORD, that He may be glorified. Then they will rebuild the ancient ruins, they will raise up the former devastations; and they will repair the ruined cities, the desolations of many generations. Strangers will stand and pasture your flocks, and foreigners will be your farmers and your vinedressers. But you will be called the priests of the LORD; you will be spoken of as ministers of our God. You will eat the wealth of nations, and in their riches you will boast. Instead of your shame you will have a double portion, and instead of humiliation they will shout for joy over their portion. Therefore they will possess a double portion in their land, everlasting joy will be theirs. (Isaiah 61:3–7)

Our life involves learning comprehensively how to move in the opposite spirit to what comes against us. The radiance of Christ within compels us to live from a higher place of identity and anointing.

In Christ, the Father grants us all things that pertain to life and godliness. We are to be filled up with all the fullness of Christ. He is not reluctant to bless us. Everything is yes and amen in Christ. He is most glorified in us when we take Him at His word.

We pray in the context of the identity that He is developing in us. He is affirming constantly who we are in Him. He grants us resources that are freely available in Jesus. To grant is to bestow favor, not as an allowance to a child but as an inheritance to the maturity of Jesus. To have our needs met is a given in the Kingdom. Our children have their needs met when they come into life. They do not earn it they simply rely on the love of those who created them. As we grow into a place of maturity in Christ we are partnering with God to learn how to cultivate the inheritance that He so gladly bestows. We do not partner with God about getting our needs met. We rest in His profound love for us as the Father. He feeds, changes and blesses us simply because we are His children. We are granted the status of much loved children. We take His loving-kindness for granted and we learn to live under His smile and be happy in Him.

As we develop in Christ, God opens up the realm of Heaven. There are new grants made available to us as we grow into our identity and destiny. He grants things to us through the promises of scripture and the word of prophecy. In partnership we learn the language of promise and how to depend upon His specific word to us.

He grants us specific things that counter what may be against us (Isaiah 61:3). The key word that accompanies grant is the word *instead*. It means in place of, as an alternative to, something against us.

When God grants something it is the end of supplication and the beginning of proclamation. We rejoice that we have received and we believe that what has been granted is now our possession. We take God for granted and He loves it! It gives Him pleasure to see us depending on His goodness in such a powerful way.

Personal Notes

Your needs are met in Jesus. Move on to discovering your inheritance. It is linked to the identity that the Holy Spirit is cultivating in you in Christ.

Maturity is knowing what needs are being met because of God's nature and how to cultivate our inheritance because of our identity in Jesus. Start a conversation with God's goodness and… take some notes!!

Failing is part of developing.
Being a failure is not.

Whenever we do something for the first time we cannot make a mistake, because we are learning. Wanting to know how to improve skills, understanding and capacity are the keys to succeeding. When we love the learning we are less likely to fail and are more capable of improving.

It's possible to fail at everything and still become the best, if we love the learning and maintain our pursuit of excellence in the process. When we don't learn we can make bigger mistakes and increase our chances of becoming a failure.

The distinction between failing and becoming a failure is blame. We blame the teacher, the trainer and the mentor for our not being able to pass a test, learn the job, or grow in life. Blaming means holding others responsible for our shortcomings. We find fault with equipment. We criticize the environment, the system, and the organization. Finding fault is at epidemic proportions in our society. Every level of human endeavor seems to have its blame culture.

If we are going to succeed we must be honest in our personal approach to learning and acquiring relevant skills and capabilities. Loving the learning means being excited about developing. It involves asking questions about how to improve. It concerns taking responsibility to upgrade. We are the common denominator in all our mistakes. Not to recognize that is to eventually become a failure.

If you are worried, apprehensive and overly concerned about failing you will not enjoy the experience of learning.

In Christ, we have closure on all our failures and are free to believe the best about ourselves. Take some ground in your new man and ask The Helper for support in your learning process. He is a genius at it!

Know your point of origin

We represent another domain, a different dimension entirely from the world around us. Our citizenship is in Heaven (Philippians 3:20). We are no longer strangers and aliens; we are fellow citizens with the saints and are of God's household (Ephesians 2:19). We are raised up in Christ to keep seeking the things that are above, where Christ is, seated at God's right hand (Colossians 3:1).

We are citizens of an all powerful realm. We represent Heaven in this world so that we can bring a manifestation of Heaven to earth. The enemy is present illegally on earth. We interact with Heaven to pour God's power into the earth. Christ is the recognized authority in the Spirit. We are here to carry out the King's command.

It is vital that we know by experience our point of origin in Christ. We are seated with Him in Heavenly places far above all other rule and authority (Ephesians 1:18–23; 2:6–7). We have power to bind and loose according to the dictate of Heaven (Matthew 16:18–19). The keys of the Kingdom depend upon our revelation of Christ and our placement in Him.

The primary issue of prayer is that if permission, promise and provision exist in Heaven for someone, then it can be brought to earth on their behalf. If it exists in Heaven it can be brought to earth and released. If something (sickness, powerlessness, *etc*) does not exist in Heaven, it can be bound on earth.

We worship from our point of origin not our earthly circumstances. When we do so we are empowered to identify the permission and loose it's expression of promise into earthbound scenarios, creating the possibility for miracles and signs of God's presence. When we pray in line with the revealed will of God, faith becomes focused and specific. Faith takes hold of God's realities.

When we operate from our place of origin in Christ we bear witness to the realm He inhabits. Heaven is our model for the Kingdom, not the activities of the local church however good they may be. How much of Heaven has God purposed to become manifest here on earth? What does fullness look like to us? It has to be more than has entered our mind and heart, beyond what we can ask or think (Ephesians 3:20).

Where the Spirit of the Lord is, liberty is our context for life and ministry. Whatever brings freedom becomes our priority. It is for freedom that Christ has set us free. In the midst of warfare, persecution and overwhelming need, knowing our point of origin is crucial. Without that revelation and experience we may be as subject to the vagaries of life as anyone else.

Personal Notes

Take time to study the scriptures in this segment. What is opening up to you regarding your point of origin?

Live as a celebrant!

Personal Notes

Does praise come easy to you? Do you have an ongoing appreciation for the Spirit of Life? Do you have to contemplate for a while to find something for which to be grateful? It's important for you to ask questions about the nature of your thanksgiving.

Celebration is what we do. We proclaim Jesus. We extol His majesty. We honor His delight in us. We applaud His sacrifice. We live in His good cheer and learn to rejoice accordingly.

Being celebrants is who we are. We live constantly provoked by joy, praise and rejoicing as a lifestyle. We count it all as joy and allow God's happiness to rule in our own lives. Celebrants focus all their attention on who Jesus is for them. He is the reason why we rejoice always and in everything give thanks.

Is it time to take your celebration from a place of doing to the point of having the lifestyle of a celebrant?

Obstacles challenge us
to make the dream bigger

27

We are governed by the passion of God for us. We are His Beloved, learning to be fully loved by Him. His passion gives us identity. We are warriors, overcomers and more than conquerors. The nature of God within our inner man of the Spirit causes us to rise up and occupy a place of anointing, power and wisdom. We are in Christ learning to become like Jesus.

As we pursue the Lord our vision begins to unfold and we set out on our journey. On this road we shall meet blessings, giftings, opportunities, presence, anointing, power and authority to name but a few! We shall also encounter great love, deep peace, fullness of joy, grace, loving kindness and favor at the very least. We will also have tribulation, opposition, warfare, persecution and various kinds of obstacles.

All of these things are good for us. Every one of these situations is designed to enable us to grow up in all things in Jesus. Each one is important and must become the subject of a dialogue with the Father. It's in our loving, prayerful conversations with God that we learn wisdom. In our relationship with God we discover how He perceives, thinks and likes to do things. The language He uses towards us is the baseline for our own proclamation. At some point along the road we will hit an obstacle. An obstruction is designed to slow us down and make us think. Left to our own devices we will simply keep going in the same direction. A barrier is really causing us to pause and take stock. There are questions that need to be asked of the Holy Spirit. What is this barrier for? It has a job to do for us and quite possibly it has things to be released to us. We must make sure that we receive what the Father wants us to appropriate.

Vision is not just about direction it is also about the height at which we are expected to travel. Everything in Jesus is about elevation. We are seated with Him in Heavenly places. We seek what is above. We come boldly into the throne room of grace (Ephesians 2, 5, 6; Colossians 3:1–3; Hebrews 4:16).

Sometimes an obstacle is placed in front of us by God for the purpose of upgrading our vision and experiencing our dream at a higher level. We can only stay on this level for so long. If our identity has not grown we must revisit our growth opportunities on this particular plane of spirituality. If we have learned something on this level but have not practiced it into a continuous experience that transforms our lifestyle, we must repeat the lesson. All we have acquired is head knowledge without a strategic life exchange in Christ.

Some obstacles appear in front of us because the Lord wants to raise our sights and develop a larger vision. The obstruction is bigger than our current experience of God. We are made small (initially) by it, but not reduced. The obstacle can only be here by permission of God, so it has to help us become what He is seeing about us. To get above any problem we must see it from a different height. We need the viewpoint from where God is standing not from where we are obstructed. We are learning to ask great questions in our fellowship with the Holy Spirit.

A particular favorite of mine is the famous: "what do You want to be for me now?" It allows us to explore God's heart towards us. What if the obstacle is present to teach us elevation? Our vision needs to go to a higher level and we must see ourselves as someone about to grow into a larger place of relationship with the Lord.

An obstruction can feel like it is challenging our dream but it's really disputing our identity. For any dream to be fulfilled we must grow into a more dynamic state of being. The challenge may be a little rough. It can feel like the dream is dying. We must remember that our chief opposer has always been a liar. Jesus is the Way, the Truth and the Life. Be led by the Spirit.

This obstacle is for our good! Therefore, we must seek God's perspective. We see more clearly when we are giving thanks. We envision more powerfully when we know that God feels challenged also, on our behalf. "What is this obstacle for? What needs to develop in me? How do I get above it? What is God's provision for me at this time?" Great questions provoke the Spirit of wisdom and revelation.

Our dream must be made bigger. The obstacle therefore is part of the enlargement process.

Personal Notes

Use the questions in this segment to begin a fresh dialogue with God. Listen closely to what God is saying. Write down the dialogue because you will need to repeat the conversation later. The words you write down will become the words of prayer, thanksgiving and rejoicing as you go through the process. In time, better questions will present themselves. Two of the really great questions were both asked on the Day of Pentecost (Acts 2:12, 37).

God has all the best thoughts!

When our mind is renewed, it is because we have accepted that God has all the best thoughts and we want them too! To be renewed in the spirit of our mind (Ephesians 4:23) is to listen to the voice of God in our heart relationship. Worship, rejoicing and giving thanks are the entry points for wisdom and revelation to come and take up residence. When we whine and complain we cannot receive the deep truth that sets us free. Self-pity guarantees that we will believe a lie and remain powerless.

The mind of Christ is compelling in its power to promote the presence of God to us. We are empowered to take our thought life to the next level of experience in God. Our thoughts are going to make or break us. They will be our divine advantage or the place of stumbling. We must learn to think brilliantly, creatively and with favor. Fortunately our Helper, the incomparable Holy Spirit, is a genius at amazing thinking. Part of His role in empowering us to become Christlike is to teach us the mind of Christ (1 Corinthians 2:16). We must not miss the opportunities to think better, bigger and more boldly.

The way we think rules our life. Our mindset can either be a fortress for the enemy or a temple for the Living God. One will imprison our spirituality; the other will set us free to govern our circumstances. Before we commit any act (good or bad) we have already entertained some thinking for a period of time. Our thinking in a situation will either take us up a level or take us down by degrees. Our experience of God cannot develop if we want new but think old.

There is only one thought to have in any situation. That is the one that Jesus is having about our identity in our circumstances. In all of our life situations we are primarily challenged to see like the Lord; think like Him; and speak into our circumstances the words of release, power and favor. Only when these three things are present and working can our behavior change to become like Him in our actions.

28

If all your thinking has brought you to a place that you don't like, it's time for a better thought. Right now the Holy Spirit, your Helper, is standing next to you. Ask Him something!

Life is emotional
and therefore Christ centered

When the Father put us into Christ, He created an internal environment within us that would always be centered around His passion for the Son. His declaration that "this is my beloved Son in whom I AM well pleased" (Mark 1:9–12), is the cornerstone of our relationship in Him. He loves our placement in Jesus!

In Christ we learn to love life in all its forms. We enjoy the journey. We celebrate who God is for us, no matter the situation. We rejoice in His name and His nature. Our passion is derived from His intention. We relax under pressure because He is our peace. We let go of fear because He is our perfect love. In troubled times we rejoice because His joy is a huge source of strength to us. Wherever we look, no matter the circumstances, He makes provision of Himself. We learn to live a life of celebration.

Because life contains many emotions, it is vital that we develop a spirituality that empowers us to be content, constant and consistent with the nature of God. Disavowing our emotional make up can lead us to a cerebral relationship that uses logic in order to attempt to experience who God is for us. When our inner man of the spirit is not partnering with the Holy Spirit we try to partner with God in our head rather than our heart. In this context we become bound by logic, which is many times more dangerous than emotion.

We partner with the Lord when we understand and receive the fullness of His passion for us in Jesus.*

We allow ourselves to become vulnerable to the joyful, restful, kind and loving nature of God. We bask in His goodness towards us. By surrendering our will to His, everything in His nature creates a God given upgrade in our personality. We become like Him in our emotions, thinking and perspective. His loving-kindness and gracious personality conforms us to His image.

---

* A fuller revelation of this is found on the CD entitled *Connecting to God's Passion* from *The Missing Piece* conference, www.brilliantbookhouse.com

What God is consistently, becomes our truest identity. Transformation comes by the renewing of our mind (Romans 12:2) in the context of being "in Christ." If our thinking is to go to the required level, our logic must give way to wisdom. Logic will keep our experience of God earthbound and shallow. Our thinking becomes conservative and our experience of God is defined by a traditional, middle of the road approach to spirituality that prevents us from encountering God in the Heavenly places. Knowing God becomes more scholastic than experiential. When head knowledge rules our academic approach to God it prevents us from having amazing, astonishing experiences with Him that transform every facet of our lives. Logic will more often talk us out of living by faith. It will rationalize our spiritual potential away from the supernatural towards a form of God that has no power.

Wisdom is the understanding of how God sees, thinks and likes to do things. It gives us a language that empowers faith and enables us to overcome in all things. When our emotions partner with wisdom we experience His passionate disposition in all our life situations. We count everything as joy and we learn the power and the beauty of rejoicing and thanksgiving. We are therefore not available for negative thinking that impacts on our emotional outlook. We learn to become glad, peaceful, unworried individuals who are basking in the cheerful nature of God, which upgrades our courage. (*Tharseo* means "to take courage and be of good cheer." It is used in: Matt 9:2, 22, 14:27; Mark 6:50, 10:49; Luke 8:48; John 16:33 and Acts 23:11.)

Rendering ourselves unemotional or controlling our feelings (so we can function) for too long is damaging to our health and relationships. Emotions are a release for us. They are a unique expression of Christ in us. They can be cathartic in our restoration and a place of celebration in life. God gave us emotions so that we could experience Him and all of His creation. In Christ our emotions have been redeemed from negativity. They are no longer subject to the world, the flesh and the devil. When our old nature was crucified in Christ our susceptibility to negative emotions died with Him (2 Corinthians 5:17).

Emotional highs are built on the stable platform of the fruit of the Spirit (Galatians 5:22–23). That means that our "high" encounter with God's passion for us is not to be followed by an emotional low. Joy, peace, rest, love and patience *etc*, when they are practiced constantly will put us into the same emotional state of being as the Lord. He is in us and we are in Him. As we practice life in Christ we do not experience every low as a trough, just more as a blip. Lows are much more shallow and temporary when experienced through God's loving nature. Weeping may last for a night (temporary) but joy comes in the morning (permanent) and kicks it out of the house (Psalm 30:5).

Obviously there are some lows that are difficult and powerful in the extreme. We hit times of intense pain and grief; personal attack and judgment; severe opposition and misunderstanding.

In those times God is our salvation. He gives us the Comforter (John 14:16–18, 26–27; John 16:7, 13–15). The Comforter empowers our emotions to not be troubled. He teaches the way of peace, joy, patience and rest. In the worst of times He guides our emotions into the grace of God so that we can experience relief and gain a release. We learn redemption as we discover long-suffering with joy (Colossians 1:11); faith with patience (Hebrews 6:12); love overcoming fear (1 John 4:18), and many triumphing over judgment (James 2:13).

Love, joy and peace are the norm for someone placed in Christ. For negative emotions we have the Comforter, who empowers our heart in difficult circumstances, so that the enemy does not get a toehold in our pain and sadness. The Comforter calls time on sorrow and weeping in order to restore us to the joyful nature of God. Being in Christ emotionally is a standard norm of Heaven and a continuous experience of life in the Spirit.

If you are currently experiencing an emotional downturn, what is God being to you right now? Is your present emotional state being orchestrated by the Comforter? How long has this persisted? Are you a victim of your emotions? Have you received wisdom and revelation for them in Jesus?

Your sorrowful emotions can never nullify the joy of the Lord. His joyful disposition must reassert itself. Your emotional downturn may have been legitimate in the beginning. The longer it continues the more it becomes illegal behavior. Only the Comforter can decide how long an opposite emotion should persist. He partners long suffering with joy because laughter bleeds away the pain and prevents it from becoming destructive.

Take stock of your emotional condition. Your emotions are in Christ, which means He rules in their outworking. Answering the above questions will get you started on a journey into an experience of the nature of God.

Miracles occur on the way

To encounter a miracle we must get beyond the limitations of conventional thinking. Miracles occur on the way. That means we must move out to meet them. God rarely sends us out with a miracle. Instead He creates scenarios for us where we learn to trust, move in faith and discover favor. Expectancy is always built on our experience of God's faithfulness.

Moses did not need the miracle of the parting of the Red Sea until he got there. Israel did not need the experience of breakfast flying in every morning until the food ran out (Exodus 14 & 16). We move out trusting God to get us there, we have specific situations where faith can overcome our lack. All obstacles are overcome in time as we stay in the favor that Jesus consistently provokes in our spirit.

The obstacles that appear at the beginning of an enterprise may only be threats. It is initial intimidation to deter us from even starting. As we move forward the real blockages will appear, and so will our provision. Next to every problem will be a solution. In the same place as the crisis will be an opportunity. When God orchestrates our path, a negative and a positive are always paired together. As we focus on the positive, trust, faith and expectancy rise up within and the negative disappears. This is the way of our Helper, the incomparable Holy Spirit. He is a genius at life in Christ. He loves our journey in the walk of faith.

In Christ we see the end product first. We see ourselves overcoming and growing in Christ because of this challenge. The primary goal of all circumstances is that we become like Jesus in relationship with the Father. The secondary purpose is that we receive under pressure and achieve the breakthrough that is present.

All that is required is that we walk forward to meet the challenge of His goodness.

Personal Notes

What kind of person do you expect to become at the end of this situation? The difference is made by your learning curve and the growth in your identity. As you focus on primary purpose the secondary objective is more easily achieved. Enjoy the journey!

Imagine God inhabiting your space!

What the Lord creates in us grows organically out of His abundance and our imagination (Ephesians 3:20). We cannot plan beauty, elegance or excellence. It is the fruit of our response to being rooted and grounded in His love. It is the normal, inevitable expression of an identity greater than our own working in us through our circumstances. We are in Christ learning to be Christlike. Christ is in us demonstrating His majesty, sovereignty and supremacy.

We have to imagine God in our space, sharing our circumstances and upgrading our identity as we travel together. If we are in Christ, so are our circumstances. Every problem reveals who Jesus is for us. He shares our space. Sometimes we step into His space and we learn to overcome step by step. It's a process. Other times He invades our space and we have a direct encounter that involves a quantum leap forward in our experience of Him. The Father decides which experience we will have. The Holy Spirit, our Helper, discloses what is to come and guides us into our personal involvement with Jesus (John 16:13–15). Jesus stands before the Father interceding for us to make it (Hebrews 7:25).

We are learning to see as God sees and become what He imagines in us (Exodus 7:1). Our circumstances enable God to upgrade us into the place of His choosing. Most of our best upgrades begin in the place of His fullness connecting with His dream for us. That dream inspires our imagination to partner with what the Holy Spirit is disclosing to us about Jesus.

What does that shared space look and feel like to you? Imagine Jesus in your space. What is He saying and doing? who are you becoming in Him? What is being upgraded in you? What can you see?

Faith is a consequence of being loved

Faith works by love (Galatians 5:6). When we learn to revel in being the Beloved of God, the action of that love promotes faith. When we receive Christ the object lesson of our life is to become rooted and grounded in the love of God. As we pursue love with God we are built up in His identity, and faith is established as a consequence. The faith of God belongs to God. Love releases the joy and peace in believing (Romans 15:13). As we learn the lessons of trust, faith and expectancy our lives overflow with gratitude for His goodness. As we have received the Lordship of Jesus we learn to walk in his supremacy (Colossians 2:5–7).

Love with faith emanates from the relationship of the Father with the Son and we are caught up in their fellowship (Ephesians 6:23; John 17:20–26). What they share in relationship we inherit and inhabit in our fellowship. The fullness of God's primary purpose in us gives us the whole range of boldness and confident access through faith in Him (Ephesians 3:11–12). The joy of faith is the consequence of becoming the Beloved (Philippians 1:25).

The nature of God provokes the enjoyment of Christ in all life situations. If nothing can separate us from the love of God, then faith, which gains its power because of love, will generate the outcome desired by God (Romans 8:37–39). When faith is required we must return to this first love. The mutual love between the Father and the Son (John 17:24) is the space that we occupy in their affection.

We must move in faith or we will begin to speculate about our circumstance. Such conjecture will open us up to theorizing about how things will turn out in our situation. When we do not know the mind of the Lord we hazard our own opinion. Guesswork inevitably leads to doubt and double-mindedness (James 1:2–8). It is extremely difficult to receive from God when we lack the wisdom of who He wants to be for us in the incident itself. We weary ourselves in speculation.

When we relax into being the Beloved we commence to be open to the primary purpose of becoming Christlike in this circumstance. The love of God touches us through primary purpose and faith becomes present. Faith is not self-generated. Love creates confidence. We believe in what God is for us now and faith rises up to experience that truth. The Spirit of disclosure (John 16:13–15) unveils to us the real truth in our present difficulty. He communicates God's intentions toward us. He imparts loving kindness and faith rises up to confess God's agenda. Finally, He makes faith more powerful than the problem and we are fully persuaded (2 Timothy 1:12). When we allow ourselves to be fully loved in each situation the consequences always lead to breakthrough.

Personal Notes

What is the assignment of the Holy Spirit in the situations that are contending against you? What is He disclosing to you? It is time for your next encounter with love and primary purpose. Enjoy His affection, receive the confidence that comes with it and the faith attached that empowers you to receive.

The humble man has an advantage over all other men... no one can put him down!

We are always victims to our own smugness, arrogance and self-delusion. Rest assured we will be taken down a peg or two if those attitudes persist in us.

Humility begins to grow in us when we learn to recognize what we are like without Jesus and what we are capable of in Him.

Humility is knowing that we have wisdom but we don't know everything. We are prophetic but sometimes God hides a thing from us. We have power but it fully belongs to Christ in us. In the Holy Spirit we can partner to create something but we are not the Creator. We know our limits but we are also unbounded in the Lord Jesus.

Humility has a foundation built upon the fruit of the Spirit. We express love in the face of opposition. We move in kindness, gentleness and patience when confronted by a mean-spirited person. When held in contempt we articulate goodness. When reviled we bless. We have a good opinion of ourselves but not higher than it should be.

Humility is not self-deprecation. To believe that in Christ we have no worth is just religious nonsense. If one of His names is Wonderful, and He is in us, what does that make us? Humility is the wisdom of knowing that we are unique, gifted and beloved of God, and accordingly, we empower others to realize their identity also.

Humility gives us the power to rise up into a high place but not become arrogant by the promotion of God. What we possess in our circumstances, of the fruit of the Spirit, will generate a humility that will bless the Lord.

In humility we are not open to the attack of the enemy. Humility guards our heart in the beauty of God. Arrogance is the erroneous belief that because we have an anointing we are better than others. Lack of humility is our undoing.

If no one can put us down, we do not have to prove ourselves. Therefore there is no need to be affronted, wounded or offended. In peace we let go of all things detrimental to us. Humility both annoys and defeats the enemy. When a hard heart comes into contact with humility it has the capacity to be softened. A soft answer turns away wrath.

Humility and gentleness will always be powerful keys that bind the enemy and loose people. They are an excellent defense against our own pride and delusion.

Personal Notes

Look back over recent experiences where you have been embarrassed and humbled. What was your response in the aftermath? What preceded your humbling? What attitude and lifestyle were you displaying? Did you reap something because of your own actions?

How will you cultivate humility in this next time frame? What price will you put on gentleness and kindness as a way of life?

34 Knowing how to receive under pressure is a great key to have in your possession.

Conventional thinking wants to receive everything in advance. However, the Lord will simply not allow us to plan everything out beforehand. We count the cost in advance but we receive our provision on the way. This is precisely why Jesus described Himself as The Way!

In order to walk by faith we must learn to trust and rejoice as our major focus of activity. Walking with God is about becoming sensitive to His name and nature. Do not try to plot a path or work out a specific strategy. God does not work to our preferences. He empowers us to live in His purposes.

Conventional thinking always tries to turn an intuition into an acquired rational deduction. When that happens all the anointing drains out of the moment. We must understand that the development of trust into faith is most crucial to the Father in every large enterprise.

Trust becomes faith, as we perceive the favor that is now present for us in relationship with the Lord. Every twist and turn on this road is concerned with our cultivating our expectation of God into a tangible reality of connection and provision.

It is a privilege to trust the Lord, so we can only do so if we are delighted at the prospect of being reliant upon His goodness towards us.

When we are not engaged in trust, we limit our possibilities instead of being enlarged by them. Each enterprise has its share of impossibilities that need converting into material resources. God has a vested interest in us learning the joy of that conversion process.

We are at our most responsible when we are trusting the Lord and seeking the next step to take in His favor. The world has nothing to teach us about trusting the Lord. It does the very opposite! The world has a business rationale that eliminates trust and faith as a possibility for living. The world is concerned with what is possible, feasible and practicable.

There is a logical, reasonable approach that refers to what may happen without prevention by serious obstacles. It seeks to eliminate the risk factor. The Lord loves obstacles because it is at these places where we discover what He wants to be for us. In Heaven's language, risk must be present so that we can grow in faith. What the world sees as things to avoid, the citizens of Heaven perceive as the only way forward into exploring the fullness of Jesus. The way of the world is to bend all possibilities into our favor by using any crafty plan and artifice to achieve the required goals. Compromise will reign instead of trust. We cut down our dream into manageable proportions so that we can achieve it ourselves. We ask the Lord to bless the way that we want to work to achieve His purpose rather than trust the ways of the Lord. We conduct a feasibility study so that we can determine the easiest way to achieve the goal. The plan that is most workable becomes the most desirable and therefore in conventional Christian thinking, the most spiritual.

In worldly terms practicable applies to that which can be done with the means at hand and with the conditions as they are. We go as far as is practicable in the circumstances. There is nothing wrong with any of that conventional thinking. It is simply not the way of the Kingdom. God loves obstacles, impossibilities and risk. Where worldly thinking seeks to eliminate those things to make it easier for us to achieve our goal; the Lord includes those things so that we can discover Him and grow in trust, faith and favor.

The primary goal of God in all circumstances is that we become like Jesus in how we perceive, think, speak and act. In Him we live, move and have our being. He allows the impossibilities so that we can be enlarged in Him.

The initial idea that we receive is seldom the real one. It's simply the precursor. It's the one that we can receive now. God gives it to us to get our attention and make us think and act differently. The initial idea is highly possible and we get excited. Actually, it is a preparation for something more but only the obstacles can reveal it to us. Obstructions are designed to school us in how to experience abundance. God uses them to train us in childlike trust, joyful faith and expectant favor. Obstacles are very important. They are excellent in empowering our rejoicing and thanksgiving which, in turn, accelerate our praying so that we ask and keep on asking, knowing that we will receive (Luke 11:9–10).

When obstacles present themselves we are learning one of the laws of life in Christ Jesus, which is: "one of the Father's great passions is His enthusiasm for our encouragement." He loves the unexpected! It is where we learn in trust to anticipate His blessing. An enterprise that can appear to be unplanned, un-designed and chaotic is actually our training and proving ground to enable us to grow up in all things.

This is the issue here! We want to plan, predict and design our way forward into accomplishing the endeavor because our primary purpose is to travel safely, without risk. The primary purpose of God however, is relational and not functional. In Kingdom thinking we need to plan, purpose and design our rejoicing, thanksgiving and praying so that we are in alignment with God's purpose. The only truly safe place is in the heart and affection of God. He loves worship and trust as a lifestyle. He adores one step at a time, relational focus. He wants us to experience Him on the journey.

It is interesting to know that at a time when the vision is bright and shiny… the process of how we can attain it is usually in conflict and chaos. We come under pressure to limit God, reduce the vision and become altogether more sensible. This is where God becomes our only source and we learn not to compromise our relationship with Him. We learn the joy of dependency instead. This is just a test. Does our intentionality to receive match God's desire to give? It is absolutely vital that we are able to receive under pressure. When the calling, dream or vision comes under threat that can often be the signal to ask God for more! When the vision is undergoing a contraction ask for an expansion. At least in worship and rejoicing we should ensure that we are fully walking in primary purpose.

Never rely on people when it comes time to believe God for finances. Many Christians develop the ministry of hints! Only God can be our source. If He uses other people that's up to Him. We, however, should not spend our time recruiting when we should be rejoicing.

Our best connection is between our favor and God's heart. We will not have to elicit support from the world if we have found favor in Heaven. Trust the Father's intuition and intention. Trust His great heart for you. He does all things well!

Personal Notes

At this time what is God's primary purpose for you? How will you develop trust into faith? What previously *future* words may have a *now* application? What is your current obstacle teaching you? Why are obstructions important to the Lord? How are you being schooled in favor? What are your current tests? Use these and other questions to open up a dialogue between your heart and the Father's.

35

Resources are attached to our identity not our circumstances

God does not allocate resources to our problems. He attaches them to our identity in Jesus. His primary purpose is in our becoming the exact likeness of the Lord Jesus Christ. We are therefore learning how to grow up in all things in Christ. In all our life events we are being schooled that God says "yes and amen" to our identity in Christ (2 Corinthians 1:20).

In Christ, the Father loves to make us big promises. Our covenant can never be detached from the majesty and sovereignty of Christ within. God works in us both to will and to do, for His good pleasure (Philippians 2:13). Big promises require huge provisions. Only in our truest identity can we experience the favor required to cash in our promises.

If we do not see ourselves as God sees us we cannot turn problems into provision. As we learn to put on Christ our persona in Heaven becomes activated in our circumstances. How we are known in Heaven becomes the seedbed for miracles to occur. When we know Heaven's perspective of us we can align ourselves with that vision and cultivate the mindset and the terminology of inheritance. Our identity in Christ has the faith we require; the creativity we need and the passion to succeed. The Holy Spirit is using all our circumstances to cultivate an impressive enlightenment and then He trains us to occupy that place in abiding presence.

This is why we are given inheritance words in scripture and also prophetic words through ministry. They are designed to expose us to our true identity and expand our partnership with the Holy Spirit.

How we are known in Heaven will expedite our deliverance from negativity, bondage from the enemy and a poverty mindset. A poverty spirit is not about economic vulnerability but is more concerned about living with meager possibilities. Our identity is our permission to step outside the confines of our personality into the fullness of God. Fullness and abundance are linked to our identity in Christ. Lack of identity means that we do not ask in faith because we have allowed for the possibility of doubt. We become double minded, unstable and have no expectation to receive from God.

When we see our true identity and begin to partner with the Holy Spirit we learn to see the resources that are attached to who we are becoming in Him.

Personal Notes

You are learning to move away from being problem focused to identity conscious. What is your process of alignment and how does the Lord develop you in this context?

36

To solve your problem
you must get above it

Vision is never just about the direction that we are moving towards on this level. It is also about the height at which we are expecting to travel in the Holy Spirit. To be in Christ is to experience His exaltation.

Everything about being in Christ is concerned with elevation. We need the spirit of wisdom and revelation in the true knowledge of the Lord Jesus, so that we can be enlightened to see ourselves in Him as the focal point of our relationship. The resurrection of Jesus to a glorious heightened state is a major key, which has a massive impact on how we live our lives in the Spirit. If He is not earthbound in His spirituality and we have been placed in him and He in us; then we cannot be subject to anything that cannot restrict Jesus (Ephesians 1:17–23; 2:5–7).

In Jesus, we are made vulnerable to an enlightened perception so powerful that we are raised up to encounter and experience a Heavenly identity that governs any earthly circumstance. We are called to know our expectations in the context of the riches of His glory in our inheritance, and the incredible majesty that is part of the relationship involving the Father with the Son. We are placed in the position of ruling and reigning with Him in this life and the one to come.

So much of our Christian experience cannot be successfully dealt with if we are always contending with it on the same level that it appears. We never deal with a negative directly. It comes at us from a lower level of existence than our placement in Christ. If we respond on the same level we become tethered to that thought and it's oppositional perception. The impact on our mental and emotional state can work against our faith, trust and enjoyment of God.

When we learn to live in the fullness of who Jesus is for us we experience His elevation. As we focus on our identity in Him the negative viewpoint becomes surplus to requirements and is dealt with indirectly in the process. The enemy wants us to deal with the negative thought. Jesus wants us to capture the thought He is releasing to us and practice obedience to it in joy (2 Corinthians 10:3–7). We do not fight against anything according to an earthly foreboding. The weapons we use emanate from a higher place of majesty and truth. In warfare it is the capture of majestic truth in our thinking that empowers our overcoming.

We are citizens of Heaven here on earth, and we draw our revelation and power from that domain (Philippians 3:20). On earth as it is in Heaven is the key to breaking through. We seek everything from the sphere of Christ's rule at the right hand of God. All our thoughts are therefore Heavenly not earthly in the context of His supremacy (Colossians 3:1–3).

It is vital we get above our situations so that we are not brought down to earth with a contrary viewpoint. If we try to deal with the negative then we become engaged in a fight we do not need to make. If our thinking has brought us to a place that we do not like then we must have a different thought. Think again! There is a better thought that can capture us into a place of obedience.

That perspective will always bring us into a place of increase. Height in the Spirit connects our vision with Heavenly places. It attaches us to authority, power and dominion as a lifestyle of enjoying the majesty of Jesus. An elevated thought life (Colossians 3:2) will always lead to fullness (Ephesians 1:22–23).

Personal Notes

Write down each negative viewpoint that is troubling your life and relationship. What is the opposite thought that can catapult you to a place of divine acceleration? Practice only dealing with the new thought and you will experience a fresh faith rising up that empowers you to realize the truth, the whole truth and nothing but the truth!

Attending is the key to hearing God

The Father's passion for our current identity is the key that unlocks our present circumstances. What is He developing in our identity and how will it impact on our personality? As we allow that thought to be cultivated in us, the situation we are currently in can begin to serve the purposes of God. As we change, resources can flow to the upgrade of our identity.

Paying attention to the Holy Spirit is most vital. Wisdom sees beyond obstructions and recognizes opportunities in the crisis. Wisdom is developed in the secret place of worship and deep thought. Meditation relies on a quiet spirit of reflection. When we meditate we consider the mirror image of Christ within and ourselves in Him. In the place of internal rest we wait patiently for the Lord. We overcome everything negative by focusing on who God is for us.

A calm spirit opens the door to presence. Stillness in our own hearts is the key to the practice of really listening. Servants of old called it "attending." They were attendants of the king or queen and had a chamber next to their living rooms in the castle.

A king would have a particular bell for each specific servant. Those attending would listen for the certain sound of their own bell. They were trained to discern the sound of the Lord. They could distinguish the particular sound that would summon them into presence. They could pick out their own sound above all others, much as a mother knows the sound of their own baby in a nursery full of crying children.

Often in times of corporate worship I hear the Lord say, "Listen to this." He will isolate one instrument in the band or one voice in a choir, and bring that sound into the foreground. I can hear and feel His enjoyment in that person playing or singing. He is attending and rejoicing. He can discern the sound of our heart among all others. He listens for us. We listen for Him.

In the busyness of life, create a clearing in the woods. A place to feel, think, relax, see clearly and relate to God. It's your own secret place. It's the place of alignment. It's the gateway into presence. The wardrobe into our Narnia.

We lose so much focus when we just run through the day. We skim the surface of all God's possibilities. Life has a feeling attached to it! It is made up of small movements that provide us with insights, experiences and opportunities. Take a moment to enjoy it! We learn peace through such times of true enjoyment. Pleasure in God is always a source of revelation.

When we attend God, we learn to wait on Him joyfully. We are present for Him. We cultivate the ground of worship as we minister to Him. Acts 13:2, as they ministered to the Lord, the Holy Spirit spoke.

When we attend, we discern His voice above all other sounds. It moves us, excites us and draws us into a more full encounter in His presence. In this place it is the easiest thing in the world to hear His voice.

Personal Notes

Creating a clearing in the woods is initially hard work. Cultivating a place of rest therefore should be done joyfully. Be delighted in the process of creating room in your heart and your day just to sit and listen. You don't have to hear anything. That's the point. We are practicing stillness. We clear away all other sounds. We mute the world around us. We relax and allow our hearts to go out to Him. Adoration is best done silently. Minister to His heart in quiet gratitude.

As that inner space fills up with peace, His still, small voice comes into the foreground. It has a musical quality, like the laughter of a small child at play. It feels like a breath of wind. Like cool water. Let it flow over you, settle your heart.

Do not try to record it in your heart, or make notes on what you are hearing. His voice initially comes to soothe our heart. He prepares us to hear His voice. In times of trouble and warfare we will be glad that we can step back into our spirit and feel the soothing sound of peace. Practice calmly and with delight.

Learn the language of Promise

As the people of God, our lives are defined by our promises, prophecies and possibilities. The Father inserts a promise into our lives lovingly so that we have His Word to hold onto when we need it. Not all promises need to be understood when they are first given, but they do need to be recorded and date stamped so we can remember it later.

At a conference where I was speaking, I expressed appreciation to the bass player in the band for his music. While I was there I heard the Lord say, "Tell him his niece will NOT die! Tell him to take this promise into her room and pray quietly and confidently like a much-loved child. His niece will not die."

I relayed the message. He looked at me blankly. A future promise when recorded now can be opened up when its time has come. I made him write it down. Apparently he had a niece that he was not allowed to see. His father was estranged from his brother and this young man had never met his uncle and aunt. Several years later his niece was in a car accident that broke almost every bone in her body and left her for dead. She was in a coma with no possibility of recovery. He got to the hospital as the priest was about to minister the last rights. Introducing himself to his uncle, he showed him the note and told him the story. The priest was called over and the story retold. The priest packed away his vestments and said, "this promise has weight, and we must allow it to do its work." The doctor, wanting to turn off life support was persuaded to wait for a day. The young man stayed in her room all night quietly praying. The next day there were signs of improvement. That day stretched into three weeks of confident praying. Each day the prognosis was better. In the fourth week she opened her eyes. After eleven weeks she left the hospital. The brothers were reconciled and the niece fully restored to health.

A promise from God is a sure thing in life. It need not be understood at the point of entry but it must be recorded and date stamped. When it is required it must be applied confidently. A promise takes away fear, weariness and worry. It's a guarantee of a future blessing.

Personal Notes

If you are serious about your walk with God you will journal. The Psalms are David's journal. They are a record of revelations, reflections, convictions and promises.

Go through your personal scriptures, prophecies and dreams. Recover the promises. If you can, date stamp them. Later on, continue to look at them and use them in your meditations and devotional times. Keep them in the forefront of your thinking, in the context of your story and journey. Are you in a place now where a previous promise may be applied to current circumstances? Sometimes we can spend time seeking a new word when a past word can be applied. God is always previous. Sometimes we have to go back to the future. A previous promise that used to be a *future* word is your *now* guarantee. Use it and rejoice.

In Him, we live, move and have our being!

Acts 17:28

We practice His presence relentlessly and with great delight. We love living in Him. We enjoy moving in Him. We adore being with Him. Simple really.

Love the learning

Life involves unrelenting learning. Every situation, problem, people difficulty and oppositional circumstance has something to teach us about God and ourselves. We learn to stand in God. We learn to press into His majesty. We learn to overcome, persist and receive under pressure. We learn to rejoice always, and in everything give thanks. We learn God's will for us (1 Thessalonians 5:16–18) in all circumstances.

Every blessing, act of goodness, expression of favor and promise teaches us about the nature of God. What we learn about His nature gradually becomes our character. There is not a single occurrence in life that does not have some learning attached to it.

It is virtually impossible to become Christlike when everything is going well. All our growth comes through learning. When people are stuck, downhearted or discouraged, it is usually a learning issue. Some learning has not taken place therefore we must repeat the cycle. The test has to be retaken later. We are held back in the previous grade until we learn enough to get onto the next level.

If we do not really learn joy, we are almost certain to become despondent. If we fail the lessons of peace, anxiety can attach itself to us. We learn trust and faith by using problems effectively. We learn how to put off the old man, be renewed in our thinking and put on the new man (Ephesians 4:20–24; Colossians 3:1–10).

Learning to think from the realm of Heaven and not the perspective of the world is a major key to growth in power. We are learning how to grow up in all things in Christ. Learning opportunities exist all around us. Make learning joyful. Wisdom accrues to people who delight in maturity.

Love the learning and avoid being angry, hurt or offended. Nasty people are our grace growers. They provide (unconsciously!) a shortcut into the nature of God's kindness, love and goodness. Learn to spot the opportunity in the crisis and take advantage.

When we fail to learn we are at a real disadvantage in life. We remain ignorant of how real growth opportunities occur. To remain unenlightened creates a distortion in our relationship with

God. People who judge can never become merciful until they learn not to judge. Similarly when we are angry we cannot learn nor release love.

Life is full of opportunities to be transformed. When we do not love the learning we make ourselves available for remedial training. We have to be corrected, which can be embarrassing. The Holy Spirit loves to teach us! If we love the learning that is present then we become teachable, trainable and joyful, willing disciples. We take full advantage of every situation. A teachable person is not available for whining, complaining or pity parties. They are too busy becoming a better individual. When we love learning to trust, we kill off anxiety, worry and doubt. It takes a long process of doubt to come to a place of unbelief in Christ. It involves lots of missed opportunities to learn trust and faith. We learned worry instead.

Failure to learn positively means we are guaranteed to learn negativity. It is psychologically easier to repeat a defeat. However, when we breakthrough in an area, the pattern of our life is interrupted. God inserts another possibility for learning. There is no breakthrough without follow through. We fight two battles over every issue. One battle to get free, another to stay free. We all know those people who won the first, lost the second and returned to a negative lifestyle. The second battle is the joyful experience of establishing our breakthrough into an ongoing lifestyle of freedom.

When we love the learning, growth is easier to acquire. We do not have time to wallow in mediocrity. If our learning capacity is attached to pain we simply will not grow. Never allow thinking to create a disadvantage. Being renewed in the spirit of our mind is made possible because our enjoyment of learning creates the inner space for transformation to occur.

The Holy Spirit is the spirit of disclosure (John 16:13–15). He loves teaching us and He enjoys our learning. He makes learning fun, interesting and powerful. He knows how to turn everything to our advantage. When we love our learning process we become truly capable of learning abundance and fullness as a way of life.

Personal Notes

Write down, here and now, the details of your current situations as an expression of what you could be learning. Take time to come before the Holy Spirit as your joyful Helper. If your love of learning matches His joy in disclosing then you can have amazing encounters and astonishing learning experiences. Enjoy!

Faith and patience always inherit the promises of God

Promises are the seedbed for miracles to occur. It is the language of God that guides our thinking and response. He loves promises, inheritance, favor and fullness. He gives His word so that the outcome may be guaranteed. This will free us up to enjoy the process of how we get there! Promises are the agenda of God to teach us fullness. There can be no experience of fullness without primary purpose being fulfilled. The ultimate goal of God is to make us in His image (Genesis 1:26–27). All other purposes are subservient to this one unchangeable desire in His heart.

Promises are designed to enable us to travel with joy and peace in believing. A promise will release us from all negativity. It gives us an agreed outcome so that we do not live under the tyranny of our circumstances. Promises enable us to explore our favor in the situation. If promise guarantees the outcome then favor endorses the process. We have an assurance of reaching our destination. How we get there is the relational issue between a loving, generous God and us.

Promises are designed to enable us to receive under pressure. They are the engine room that keeps us moving forward regardless of oppositional forces. They empower us to abide in His nature. They remove worry and anxiety as a possibility for living and enable us to live in His gracious, good news.

Promises will develop our trust into faith. A promise is the key of focus that enables us to become fixed on what God is doing rather than what the problem is saying. Every situation has a voice that communicates something to us from the world around us. A promise is the voice from Heaven, which if we focus on it, will drown out every other sound. Proclamation is the loudest vocal sound, because at it's very center is the exuberance of joy. When we have a promise we gain huge confidence in speaking it aloud joyfully in our circumstances. We rejoice and give thanks! The sound of exuberant praises gives us enthusiasm and energy in the Spirit.

It is important that we are not slow to learn the lesson of faith with patience. It is the only way to continuously inherit in all the levels of life in Christ (Hebrews 6:12). Faith can only go to its required height when it is combined with patience. We live in a result driven world of instant gratification. Sadly, this has permeated the Body of Christ. We encounter the world system in the church rather than the Kingdom of Heaven. Life in Christ comes to us from an altogether different domain. Some situations can be changed immediately with a word of authority. Others change gradually through patient endurance. Both are required to enable us to become Christlike.

It is the combination of faith and patience that provides us with an irresistible guarantee that will release provision at the required time. When we wait on the Lord, the world cannot push us around with its timetable. Impatience is always our undoing. We allow ourselves to be pressured by people and events. Patience is not just a place we live in when tribulation occurs. It is the habitation of God in which we live, move and have our being.

Impatience gives the enemy power to disrupt our circumstances. We can be easily beaten from within if we lack the stamina to endure. Living from Heaven to earth does not allow for frustration. If it does not exist in Heaven in Jesus, it cannot have life in us! We can bind what does not exist in Heaven (*i.e.* frustration), and loose what Heaven enjoys (patience).

Patience is calm endurance; an uncomplaining nature; diligent application, and tireless stamina. God does not grow weary. We live in him learning to persist in His nature above the circumstances of life. We do not merely persevere in our circumstances. That is the consequence of faithfulness. Our primary purpose is to become like Jesus. In this regard, learning to persist in the fruit of the Spirit is the important key in our development.

We can exult in the affliction, ordeal, trouble, hardships, pain or adversity because they all develop proven character and Jesus (Romans 5:1–4). The trial is the key to growth. Patience is the key to faith.

Personal Notes

"You have need of patience so that when you have done the will of God, you may receive what was promised" (Hebrews 10:36–39). Do not shrink back from primary purpose.

Study the opposite of patience, and then study patience itself. One provides power that works for us, the other power against.

What promises do you have already in your possession? They are our necessary focus in current circumstances. What is that voice speaking out in your situation?

The fruit of the Spirit is our Divine Advantage

We are in Christ learning to live from Heaven to earth in our salvation experience. We are learning the joy of the Lord in all circumstances. Joy is unconfined delight. It is His gladness rooted in His majesty. His cheerful disposition is grounded in the omnipotence of His own strength. His joy becomes our strength! His omniscience is the origin of His good pleasure. He not only knows everything, He also knows how to live in everything. His presence fills all in all because He knows what He wants to be for us in every circumstance.

We are in the business of enjoying how to live in His presence. Primary purpose demands that the most important focus in every situation is that we are made in His image (Genesis 1:26–27). The key to every circumstance is presence. The key to presence is focus on the aspect of God's nature that He wants to develop in us through the situation in hand. All other objectives are subservient to primary purpose.

We are being schooled in the ways of peace, rest and joy. Every single situation is concerned with training in the nature of God. The first requirement in all circumstances cannot be the resolution of the problem. Primary purpose is concerned with using everything to become like Jesus. In this context for life we are advantaged in every possible way. Life on earth is designed to showcase our new DNA. We are new creations in Christ: all the old way of focus has passed away, everything has become new (2 Corinthians 5:17). Our key focus is the nature of God.

We lead with His nature. "The fruit of the Spirit (Galatians 5:22–23) is love, joy, peace, patience, kindness, goodness, faithfulness, gentleness and self control. Against such things there is no law!" Nothing can overcome the nature of God. Nothing works against the nature of God. The fruit of the Spirit is the very definition of presence. It is the first line of defense in warfare, and the catalyst for overcoming in the beauty of God. His great love provides all our defining moments and underpins our most profound learning experiences. Everything that God is in Himself is what sets us apart to be different in the world. His nature empowers our faith and trust.

The fruit of the Spirit is a constant, not a variable. It is a fixed lifestyle not a fluctuating, situational charisma that is only developed by events. We are becoming faithful to the nature of God. "My heart is fixed o God, my heart is fixed," cried the psalmist (Psalm 57:7). Life in the Spirit is not spasmodic; it is as unchanging as God. It is not an erratic influence but a permanent disposition. Loosing the fruit of the Spirit in our lives empowers us to become like Jesus in inclination and character. In the fruit of the Spirit we learn the divine advantage of our DNA in Jesus. When we practice the fruit of the Spirit we cannot become negative, weary, worn down and despondent. Instead the fruit of the Spirit enables us to take advantage of every situation that arises. We can afflict the enemy with our DNA in Christ. It is where we pressure the enemy through our identity.

The Father always pairs our circumstances with a particular fruit of the Spirit. We have long-suffering attached to joy. (Colossians 1:11) Trials are yoked with joy; faith with patience (James 1:2–4). Peace is paired with trouble (John 14:27). Peace guards our heart and minds (Philippians 4:4–7). We overcome evil with goodness (Romans 12:21). Love casts out fear (1 John 4:18). Kindness is particularly effective against all forms of negativity (1 Peter 2:1–3). Gentleness is teamed with the restoration of sinfulness (Galatians 6:1–2). God has assigned aspects of His nature to every circumstance of life. Primary purpose is bound to every purpose of the enemy resulting in Divine Advantage for all God's people.

When we focus on God's nature as our first response to everything, we receive the key that opens up the circumstance to God's blessing and favor. We are in him learning how to persist in His nature, rather than trying to persevere in the situation. Continuing in primary purpose puts us above the circumstance. We overcome when our goal to become like God is greater than our need for resolution of the problem.

When God ties a problem to a particular aspect of His nature, He is putting an important key into our hand. He is detailing the process of how we get to the outcome. He is defining what He wants to teach us about His nature. For example take 1 John 4:16–19:

> 16 We have come to know and have believed the love, which God has for us. God is love, and the one who abides in love abides in God, and God abides in him. 17 By this, love is perfected with us, so that we may have confidence in the Day of Judgment; because as He is, so also are we in this world. 18 There is no fear in love; but perfect love casts out fear, because fear involves punishment, and the one who fears is not perfected in love. 19 We love, because He first loved us.

When fear is present in us, God attaches it to perfect love. When we focus on fear we are undone by it. When we focus directly on love then fear is dealt with as a consequence. The stronger our attachment to love the more mature we become in this aspect of God's nature. We live in the fruit of the Spirit that is assigned to the problem; not the problem itself. As we persist in the designated fruit, the problem comes under the rule of our internal DNA in Christ. We find the appointed fruit that is present; use it to become Christlike; and we banish the problem indirectly.

All the most wonderful things of God come to us via testing. We are in a constantly refining process, where only the heat changes. The best way to live is to be focused on the nature of God as the goal of everything. Do not stray from primary purpose, which is to become conformed to the image of Jesus. Cultivating His nature is one of the primary keys of the Kingdom. When we combine negative situations with the fruit of the Spirit it is so we can allow our internal DNA to rise up within and overcome. We learn to persist in God's nature not persevere in the problem.

The real test is not the resolution of the situation (that's the by-product); it is the development of God's nature in the fruit of the Spirit.

In your current situations what fruit of the Spirit has been assigned to each difficulty? Please note that joy has been attached to everything! (James 1:2–3)

The aspect of God's nature assigned to your problem details the process of your journey. What is God revealing to you now, concerning what He wants to be for you?

The mind of Christ
gives us a different language

We have grown up in the world system of perception, thinking and language. We have grown accustomed to our thinking being derived from the world, the flesh and the devil. When we connect with Jesus we come under a mindset from a different domain. The mind set on the flesh is hostile to the majesty of God. The mind-set of the spirit brings new life and tremendous peace (Romans 8:5–8; 14, 12:2). Transformation can only come when our thinking is being consistently, powerfully changed.

The wisdom of Heaven must replace the wisdom from the world (James 3:13–15). We do this by a process called reframing. Framing is an artistic skill that many artists do not possess. They can paint a brilliant portrait but choose an unsuitable frame that works against the portraits true beauty or excellence. In another way a wonderful frame can make an average portrait seem more amazing.

The way we think about something can similarly frame the way we see something. Our thinking can put our perception into a place where we cannot have a breakthrough encounter in life. People want new but think old. We are a new creation but our thoughts, perceptions and language are experienced from the old creation, not the new man in Christ. Conversations are riddled with old man perceptions and mind-sets because our thinking is not sanctified in Christ.

Our thinking is still a stronghold of the enemy that must be systematically destroyed so that our new thinking takes us to the place of renewal and obedience (2 Corinthians 10:4–6; Ephesians 4:20–24). We must think from the new man in Christ.

We have access to a hidden wisdom in Christ that is not part of this worldly mindset. As we receive it we enter into a deeper, more glorious relationship with God. We learn to think, perceive and speak from a position of radiant knowledge. This wisdom releases to us an understanding of what God is doing in our lives and how He is preparing us to walk in His brilliance. The Holy Spirit, our specific Helper, constantly searches the depths of God and reveals to us vital truths that upgrade the quality of our spiritual experience. We are meant to receive revelation of what truly belongs to us in Christ and the anointing to grow up into Christ in all things. This wisdom of the new man is the subject of all our conversations. We have the favor of God to spiritually appraise all our thoughts so that we can be instructed by the Mind of Christ (1 Corinthians 2:6–16... *please read!*).

If we do not reassess our thinking in line with the internal presence of Jesus, we cannot turn any single encounter with God into an ongoing lifestyle experience. We become, by default, people of visitation rather than a habitation of God by the Spirit. The result of that mindset is that we develop a religious culture geared more to our performance rather than our placement in Jesus. We are seekers of God but our un-redeemed mindset does not allow us to experience the fullness of His truth (2 Timothy 3:7).

When we are stuck in a place of negativity that makes us feel powerless and frustrated, we need to have access to a new way of thinking about our perceptions. Too much pastoral ministry is based around working on the old nature rather than replacing it with the new man and developing the thinking that comes out of that position. The new man in Christ has a completely different thought about our current problem. When we change the frame we have a different encounter with God. If something is limiting us, our new man can reframe it to a place of what is now possible. Spiritual appraisal allows us to have fresh encounters and life-changing experiences.

The Holy Spirit loves to take the things of Jesus and make them new and real for us. In Christ we are never stuck, nor imprisoned by a thought. Reframing is a key that unlocks our life to the wisdom from above. This wisdom creates a place of purity in our thinking that upgrades our mindset to peace, gentleness and merciful perspectives. We are no longer prone to doubt and we do not say one thing but think another (James 3:17).

When we are present/past in our thinking and lifestyle we have a spirituality geared to only seeing problems. The unexpected can often be received as a problem rather than an opportunity. Problems require help, or solutions. A mindset on problems can take us into a functional place with God where the resolution of a difficulty is our priority; but an upgrade in our thinking may be His agenda for us.

Framing an event as a problem can take us away from wisdom and give us a language that limits our faith in God.

"I can do all things in Christ, who strengthens me," is a re-framed thought that opens up all the possibilities of God. The world is geared to problem solve at every level of human experience. In Christ the problem of ourselves has been dealt with on the cross. We need to become aware of which self is talking in our current situation. Is it our old self or our new self?

God has taken all things that were against us in the old self and crucified it with Jesus. What is your new, true, real self saying? "Set your mind on things about not on things on the earth. For you have died and your life is hid with Christ in God," (Colossians 3:2–3).

A problem frame means that we do not see what God has done, or is doing. A problem frame also looks to put a fault somewhere in the picture so that someone else can be blamed. When we step out of our own picture our identity has nowhere to go but down.

When we are learning to be present/future in our thinking we can learn to frame prophetically. That is, we look at our situation in the light of prophetic words, promises and life-giving scriptures that have been inserted into our lives in a previous time by the Holy Spirit. Those words can start to have an immediate impact on our identity. If a person with the mindset of a wimp receives a prophetic word that he/she will become a warrior, then the process of transformation comes by the renewing of the mind. We must empower that person to begin to reframe their thinking through a warrior rather than a victim mindset. Every problem, difficulty and adversarial situation therefore now provides training in warrior thinking and identity. On their journey from slavery in Egypt to the conquest of Canaan, Israel needed to reframe their thinking and identity from a rabble of slaves to a disciplined army who could take territory. Failure resulted in hundreds of thousands of people denying themselves a dynamic new inheritance.

The future that God connects us to in the present demands a new perspective. Prophecy gives us an outcome that therefore guarantees the process. Asking "who is God for me now?" is an outcome frame. "What future do I really want?" empowers us to a different destination. Asking people if they have a prophecy or promise can open up the present/future for a fresh dialogue that enables us to explore something new and more vital. Promises allow us to experience God's intention (Jeremiah 29:11).

Moses held up a problem frame regarding his speech impediment, which, he felt disqualified him from the role that God intended (Exodus 4:10). The resolution of that difficulty came in God's reframing of the identity of Moses in Exodus 7:1. "See, I make you as God to Pharaoh and Aaron shall be your prophet." A spiritual appraisal occurs when our viewpoint on something is the same as the Lord's. A prophetic frame gives us a more dynamic outcome. What has God said? We have to see it! Then we have to see ourselves becoming it and doing it.

A prophetic word re-frames our thinking; upgrades our vision of ourselves, and gives us a new language for our identity.

In Christ we have the "newness of life" frame (Romans 6:3–11; Galatians 2:20; Philippians 4:13). We get to imagine Jesus within. How would He see this circumstance? How would He engage with it?

Jesus within will cause us to see things differently. He gives us more than just an interpretation of something. He is the Way, the Life and the Truth! (John 14:6) His viewpoint and passions for us create a whole new language with which we can explore the situation. All things that were impossible before are now made possible in Him. In Jesus we are being quietly, lovingly and joyfully faced up to a newness of life. We have God's absolute permission to consider ourselves dead to an old man mindset and to be alive to Him instead (Romans 6:11). The Holy Spirit is training us to explore new ways of becoming different in our thinking. We have the mind of Christ. We are transformed by the renewing of our mind (Romans 12:2). Reframing is a wonderful, spiritual exercise in thinking in line with our new man in Christ. From that place of being renewed in the Spirit of our mind, we get to develop mind-sets and activations that are rooted in the reality of Christ within. Our language reflects the reframing of our thought life. "I can do all things in Christ, who strengthens me" (Philippians 4:13).

The growth of our identity depends upon our mindset changing; the growth of our personal perspective, and the development of a new language in which to express all that God wants to be for us. A newness of life frame opens up all the possibilities of the Kingdom invading our time-space world with the radiant good news of the Gospel.

Personal Notes

Where have you become stuck in your thinking, perception or language? What are the opportunities opening up for you now? How will you develop your newness of life frame? What spiritual appraisals are you engaged in upgrading?

Your intimacy is intimidating

When the Father placed us into Christ, He put us into a position of intimate affection between Him and the Son. In this incredible place of emotional attachment we are allowed to experience the intimate connection in their relationship. We encounter their unique Oneness. We are lovingly confronted by the radiance of their shared glory. We participate in First Love. The love that they have had since before the foundation of the world (John 17:20–26). The love with which Jesus is loved by the Father must also be in us.

The goal of God is that we become rooted and grounded by ongoing experience in their love for each other. He desires that we fully understand who we are in the context of First Love. In every direction and on each level of life experience we are graced to partake of a love so huge and all encompassing that we are filled up by its fullness (Ephesians 3:16–21). There is a love, which overwhelms every kind of knowledge and experience. Imagine a love so great it makes us inarticulate with wonder!

In the context of such an awe-inspiring mutual affection we are encouraged to ask for things beyond what we can reason out and adequately express. In the power of the love that is placed deep within our spirit we discover a form of prayer that has no words. We reach the place of His incredible passion, and the delight we feel in Him causes all manner of holy desires to be articulated through intimate worship.

There is a close familiarity between the Father and the Son, which we can receive. The Holy Spirit guides us into an internal relationship so powerful that its fullness governs our lives! We experience that cherished trust in the Godhead. We become deeply confident in our attachment to First Love. In our innermost being we are lovingly bombarded by the radiant nature of deep, abiding, personal, limitless, relentless and overwhelming passionate adoration that exists in the community of the Father, Son and Holy Spirit. It is beyond comprehension. It must be both encountered and experienced fully in our ongoing lifestyle.

In the context of that love, our intimacy becomes the most intimidating thing about us to the enemy. In the passion of First Love we receive influence with power. We become an experienced confidante of the Spirit of Disclosure (John 16:13–15) who loves to reveal all things. When we are constantly touched by the deep passions of God's love we are wholly set free from any negative. The prince of this world has nothing on us (John 14:30). The awe and reverential fear of the Lord governs our life and strikes fear into the heart of the demonic. The enemy is rendered vulnerable to the majesty of God's love radiating through an individual. He is compelled to obey the word of the Lord. He is a created being ordained to serve the purposes of God from the beginning. Nothing has changed! He is compelled to serve Jesus.

Intimacy with God makes the enemy intimidated. This place has been set aside for us in Christ. Learning to abide there is the seat of power in warfare.

What is the next level of your intimate affection with God? What old negatives are being targeted in First Love?

We never exit worship

Passion is the discovery of what is true and empowering about God's personality. This touches our emotions and releases revelation. Key insights are released and become possibilities that empower our faith. Worship in that context is the permission to become lost in the rhythm of God's heartbeat.

The Father is never passive in worship. He is actively engaged with us. We allow our hearts to go out to Him. We desire His company in worship. We reach out to Him with everything we have. We intentionally use the truth of His nature to touch Him. We celebrate all that He says about Himself. We find favor in His sight and we revel in who He is for us. We discover that His kindness, love, generosity and joy are unbounded towards us. We can therefore rejoice in His mercy and give thanks for unending grace.

His delight over us turns into our delight over Him. Our heart moves in tune with His. We lose our self-consciousness about what we are not by basking in who He is for us. True worship takes us to the resurrection side of the cross. In high praise we ascend to a High Place. Worship has to be about touching Heaven. It is about our imagining our place in Jesus around the throne. It is a life enhancing experience. It transforms us by empowering us from within. We draw back from the outer power of the soul so that we may feel the presence of God in the inner man of the spirit. Our innermost being is continuously ever-present with God. He lives in our spirit.

Worship enables us both to reclaim and then maintain our inner territory. It opens our heart and renews our mind in Jesus. We never worship the same way twice in succession. There is no system to intimacy. It is not about what we are doing, but about what we are allowing to happen in our hearts.

Worship comes to us in the form of God's favor towards us in Christ. It flows with us and moves through us. Worship is a Person wooing us. As we respond, we enter into a relationship with God that is intimate and bold. True worship leaders are not choirmasters. They do not lead singing. They are caught up in their own movement. The Lord plays their heart like an instrument. In that place of intimacy He uses their heart to attract, inspire and compel people to respond.

Worship is always different because we are continually in discovery. It allows us to explore the Father's heart for us. Sometimes, we begin from a place we know. A particular truth that we celebrate about Him. At other times we take a run and jump off a cliff into the security of His heart. Sometimes, when life is against us, the Comforter comes and embraces us. We slow dance in His deep, compassionate understanding and we are healed, restored and strengthened. The memory of His amazing and compelling intimacy stays with us for days afterwards. The enemy is lost to us and cannot take advantage of our pain. He cannot penetrate such comfort.

Intimate worship is a powerful restoring touch that draws us up and out of ourselves into the majesty of the Lord. Real intimacy remains enshrined in our memory banks. It can be called up in moments of battle, rising up within us. The touch and the feel of God that we have experienced leads us into a fresh encounter with His glorious nature. Encounter begets ongoing experience, which brings us to fresh encounter. His steadfast love never fails. It is new every morning. His mercy is endless. We are never alone. He is everywhere in and around us. Intimacy means that we never exit, nor rule out the Father's delight in us. His faithfulness is so overwhelming; it actually empowers us to become brilliant. When we relax into His faithful affection every hardship slips away from us and we are clean and strong.

We never exit worship. It is a melody that is either in the foreground or the background of our hearts. When it comes to the fore, we must give ourselves to it generously. Allow the moment to take us over for however long the Spirit desires. We must remember that worship is His dance and He must take the lead. We move to His tune. All creation worships continuously.

Creation was made from a word spoken by the Father. A word is a sound that has creative significance and meaning. Creations moves to the rhythm of His heartbeat. That sound is all around us.

Whenever we connect with the inner man of our spirit we hear the sound of God moving within. Stillness is about becoming quiet within so that we can hear the sound of worship and join in with what all creation is always doing.

When God inhabits our spirit the rhythm of His heartbeat and the sound of His joyfulness is implanted within our hearts. "Rejoicing always" is possible when we connect within to the sound of intimacy. We each have a certain sound, like an instrument in an orchestra. The Father plays our heart through the Holy Spirit who loves to move us in the rhythm of Heaven. Everything sings to the tune of His heart. When we are moved by love our hearts vibrate to the sound of His delight, and we too become delighted. It becomes our joy to delight ourselves in the Lord (Psalm 37:4).

Personal Notes

What is your sound in worship? What is your next level of worship that must be embraced? Do your praise, rejoicing and thanksgiving need a refreshing upgrade? What would that look like for you?

Passion creates focus

Passion never allows you to see yourself as a failure. Everything is useful in our development. Mistakes, humiliations, defeats and obstacles are as valuable as success, achievement, victory and breakthrough. Passion wastes nothing. Passion always learns and always overcomes. Passion is belief in action.

What if failure has nothing to do with passion? What if failure is only tied to goals and ambitions that are not a part of our identity or destiny? We fail when we fall short of a specific goal.

What if passion doesn't require specific goals? What if it is so much more powerful than that? Passion is about how we live in our hearts, each day. Passion gives us focus... not just on where we are going but the manner in which we get there. Passion loves the journey! Goals are all about destination and outcome. Focus will make sure we arrive; passion will get us there in the best possible shape because we will have thoroughly enjoyed the journey with all its twists and turns.

If all we have are goals, we may not make it. We will use ruthless determination rather than passion. If we do make it we will leave a trail of discarded people, broken promises and distress behind us. Passion arrives whole in nature, having enjoyed the journey. Passion allows us to travel differently. Passion and focus allow us to build trust and faith. Passion and focus develop confidence. They open us up to see the prophetic. They provide rest and security that allow us to see the invisible, become aware of all the possibilities around us, and take risks happily in Jesus' name.

Ambition and goals can make us self-centered. Passion and focus allow us to include others on our journey. Often God has brought others into my life so that He can help them through me. My passion focused on helping them and as they prospered, so did I! Passion and focus help us to sow and reap. As I gave, so I grew. Being outward looking, including other people in my focus actually became a shortcut for me to experience.

Passion and focus enable us to enjoy every day and every circumstance. We learn to love the hand of God. This kind of living empowers us to grow. Every day is exciting. We grow in grace and favor. We practice our peace, we love our life, and we enjoy the journey.

Ambition and goals require great mental strength. They demand that we live with blinkers to narrow our vision so that all we can see is the goal. We live from our head not our hearts. We get tougher so we can stay the course longer.

For every person who achieves their goal there are tens of thousands who don't. Ambition and goals suck the enjoyment of living now, out of us. Only the mentally strong can live that way. Study the lives of ambitious people and you will mostly discover a story of pain and loss. They arrive at the top, broken and devoid of joy, peace and loving relationships.

To arrive at the top is one thing... to stay there demands more ruthless determination and an iron will. These people are powerful but not enjoyable. Their destructive tendencies will continue to use people. To avoid failure they may choose to do anything... illegal, evasive or unpalatable. Lives can become fraudulent when we see people merely as objects to serve us or obstacles that prevent us from achieving our goals. Ambition can kill. Passion creates life.

Personal Notes

What passions have you ignored in your development as a person? What goals have you made and how do they relate to the real you that you were created to be?

If you do not fit into the world that you have allowed to form you, maybe it's time for a rethink?

A truth which is not
practiced denies God
the right to upgrade your
experience of Him.

Personal Notes

A truth not practiced is merely true for us. We remain bound because only the truth can set us free. A truth believed but not experienced has no power to renew or upgrade our fellowship with God.

What truths have you believed but not experienced to the point of being transformed?

The key is the test

People who are always looking for a shortcut seldom pass the test of life. The test is the shortcut. The key is the test that God gives us so that we can receive, become and inherit what He sees over us. Testing is always linked to the development of our obedience (2 Corinthians 2:9; 10:5).

What the Spirit discloses must be proven in us. All revelation is tested so that our experience can empower us to occupy the place that God has set aside for us. The difference between remaining a child and becoming an adult are the tests that we must embrace along the way. Failure is caused by our lack of learning. We do not see this incident as a test so we do not grow in this adversity, which means it must be repeated.

We cannot fail the tests of God but we will get to take them again, and again, and again. Until we pass! The test is the key to growth. Are we willing to become obedient and trustworthy? Jesus learned obedience by the things He suffered (Hebrews 5:8). We must do likewise. Whatever keys of the Kingdom that God wishes to bestow on us will form a vital part of our testing and proving ground. It is important therefore that we pay attention to our burdens in the Spirit. Whatever we feel strongly about will be tested in us first. We are tested personally by the freedoms that God wants us to impart to others.

Our tests are everywhere, everyday. Our words, actions, promises and integrity are tested constantly. Our determination and resolve in life and ministry are tested for authenticity.

The key is the test and the test is the key.

Look back over the past three months. What tests in relationships, word and action presented themselves to you? Did you pass them or are they still current?

In long-standing relationships what promises have you not fulfilled? What is the nature of your inauthenticity?

God meets us more in our imagination than He does in our logic

To move in passion… to live passionately… we must develop intuition. Intuition is a state of mind and heart that takes us into a higher place than logic or reason. Logic and reason are base camp one on the climb up Everest. They must be left behind if we are to reach the summit of real thinking. God is much too clever to be an intellectual. He lives in a high place of wisdom. Wisdom is far superior to knowledge. It is an affair of the heart. When our mind and heart combine we receive enlightenment. This is a way of thinking that is present/future—wrapped in peace, allowing for joy and full of radiant intuition. It allows us to operate from a place in the spirit where faith is easy and we have already overcome. Logic and reason make the best of external circumstances. They calculate odds and supply us with a best possible solution, based on information available. Logic and reason make us poor and keep us earthbound in our thinking. As spiritual beings we are allowed to touch Heaven in Jesus' name. We are seated with Christ in Heavenly places. We are practicing an ascended lifestyle. We live from Heaven to earth. We are therefore above certain things already.

We live above the enemy not under his power. We have access to a way of seeing, thinking and experiencing that is unlimited by rationale.

God gave us a way of thinking that is unlimited. Ephesians 3:20 states: "Now to Him who is able to do far more abundantly beyond all that we ask or think, according to the power that works within us…"

What is it that is abundantly beyond all we can think of? What is the power within that can do that? What is beyond rational thought?

It is our imagination. God gave us imagination so that we could escape logic as a rationale for life and living. Think of every invention, every advance in technology… none of them began in logic. Someone, somewhere, saw something that could not be seen and then made it visible. It's logical for a wooden ship to float, but an iron one? The first telegraph. Internal plumbing. Radio. Television. Space travel. Telephones. Computers. The Internet. X-Ray machines. Photography. The list is enormous. All those things came from imagining. It's even called *imagineering*. Seeing an image and making it real and discovering in the process how God makes science work. It's the science of how God bends the universe to His will. How the real world is based on God's intuition, wisdom, will and His essential nature.

God meets us more in our imagination than He does in our logic. He is our imagination and intuition. Wisdom is the spiritual way to think. Imagination, not logic, is the doorway to practicality.

Logic is not reality. It's just a non-intuitive version of it. Imagination creates. It breaks the limits of possibility. We think in a different space.

Passion, creativity and dreams all arise out of our intuition about ourselves, and the permissions we have from the Father. They connect our present with the future so that we can see what the Father is seeing about who we are now and who is emerging in us in the future. These thoughts are rooted in our imagination through the prophetic input of the Holy Spirit.

When God invited Moses to "See, I have made you as God to Pharaoh and Aaron shall be your prophet" (Exodus 7:1), it was an invitation for Moses to imagine. He got to see something that had not physically occurred yet, but was nevertheless a done deal in the heart of God. Dreams, visions and prophetic language enable us to escape the crushing power of earthbound logic and experience God in the creative power of His imagination.

Personal Notes

When you dream, what do you see? When you sit quietly in the presence of God what opens up to you?

Take some moments to escape the ordinary grind of logic and rationale, access the bigness of who God is for you. What can you see in His relationship with you?

Take a passage of scripture that the Holy Spirit has made compelling and real to you. As you read and ponder over it, what do you see yourself becoming in the light of this word? Write it down. Now imagine that happening. What do you see now?

This is how God teaches us to see what He sees when He looks at us.

Reinvention has many layers

Poverty is not economical. It is the acceptance of meager possibilities. There is a poverty of thinking, imagination, passion, courage, vision and the will to succeed. We become limited by our fears. Fear of failure, change, looking foolish and being criticized make us dormant and inactive. The fear of man is one of the most debilitating phobias available to us in our experience of the world.

We can convince ourselves of our lack of resources but the reality is that we do not go out to meet them. In our anxiety, we wait for them to come. We are the people of God so we can never allow ourselves to be defined by externals... what shall we eat or wear (Matthew 6:31)? Our bank balance has nothing to say about what God will do. We are defined internally by the nature of God towards us. He has no restrictive labels for us. He empowers us to believe in Him as He believes in us. When we believe that He is with us then faith ruses up and we believe in ourselves too.

People need to understand identity and destiny. As part of that development we cultivate an environment that empowers them to step into all that He wants to be on their behalf. The questions we must ask: Are our personal assumptions of ourselves self-defeating? Or, do they inspire us to attempt new things?

A poverty mindset diminishes our personality and prevents us from realizing our truest identity in Jesus. It starves us of hope and vision. We then define ourselves by what we cannot do. We follow the path of least resistance because we do not realize that it is the resistance we encounter that empowers us to succeed. We must have something big to overcome. The starting point to victory is recognizing our present giant and what it will develop in us. Personal assumptions can either be destructive or productive to our development. Impoverished assumptions are not the truth. Only the truth can set us free.

When we know our permissions, we will also discover the current portion of our inheritance. If we are too focused on finances at the beginning of an enterprise, we may well not be seeing the bigger picture. The Father will always show us the truly impossible element of the dream, His calling. When we depend upon His passion for us we get to also joyfully confess that He is our full provision. If He is not under attack then our resources are safe in Him. We rest in our confession of Him. We use our declaration of His intentionality towards us to celebrate His passion. We must have the peace of God so that our proclamation of Christ can become the focal point of our believing in the circumstances. The enemy is defeated by our rest and confidence in Jesus.

In the beginning there is always God. At the start of any enterprise, we must not focus on the task ahead; first we must upgrade our relationship with the Lord.

We strengthen the foundations of our relationship with the Godhead by seeking a place of prayerful upgrade with each member. We increase our celebration in terms of rejoicing and thanksgiving. In this place of upgraded presence we are given clarity about God's intention. We are able to come to a fresh place of rest and confession. We become aware of our role in the process of our development.

It is in these areas that we improve our partnership with God. If we are scrambling to make ends meet, we are not partnering with the Father. The pressure of survival will cause us to focus too much on the present. Therefore, we do not look forward enough to develop a vision for the future, because that seems to us to be a luxury. Abundance surely means that we have the luxury to partner with the God of the future?

Reinvention has many layers. It covers our personality, attitude, focus, renewed mind, communication, faith and identity. To name but a few! Everything we are in ourselves is subject to adjustment. We are learning to listen for the future in all our present conversations. To be prophetic means that we discern emerging possibilities before they become visible. In the process of reinvention, we will close the gap between vision and success by the determination of God to make us in His image, and by our joyful willingness to take our full responsibility in that process.

Personal Notes

What are the basics that you need to return to if you are to successfully reinvent your identity in Christ?

What poverty thinking is holding you back in your vision of the future? What are you listening for in regard to your own future?

If you do before you get it, what you would do if you had it, you will be sure to get it!

Abraham believed in His inheritance and went out to find it, not knowing where he was going (Hebrew 11:8).

Sarah believed that God was faithful and received the ability to conceive, beyond her physical ability to reproduce.

Joshua believed the prophecy about Jericho's walls falling down and by faith marched around it in obedience to God (Joshua 6).

When we believe but don't act, we are doubting and being influenced by our circumstances (James 1:6–8). It leads to instability and double thinking.

When we believe in God's capacity we must step out in His ability. God believes in us and has given us the means to envision Him in action before the event.

What words have you received in the past that can be applied in the present?

What future words do you have in your possession? Are the roots of their success being planted in your current circumstances?

What does He want you to believe about Him in the here and now?

In Christ we are always reconciled to our potential

When Jesus is irresistible to us, the life that He generates will immobilize the enemy. When our flesh is overthrown, the enemy is dispossessed. Everything that is positive towards us has the opposite consequence for our opponents.

The keys of the Kingdom come when we live an ascended lifestyle. When we trust the nature of God to us, we can begin to trust His nature in us. As we relax into His nature He comes through us to confront the enemy and loose our circumstances to discover His purpose. When we trust in the nature of God, our inner man is open to outrageous possibilities.

It is so important that we really understand the bigness of God's heart towards us. It is the starting point of our favor. The Holy Spirit is given to us so that we might know the things freely given to us in Christ. His role is to teach us abundance. In order for us to learn fullness we must eradicate a poverty mindset. In Christ, we must always be reconciled to our potential. We are all born again into the potential to become like Christ.

The way to unlock that potential is to create the same environment on earth that exists in Heaven. Create the atmosphere within for growth to occur. Farmers do not grow crops; they prepare the soil. They look after the land and they plant seed. Similarly, we prepare and keep our hearts with the help of the Holy Spirit, who plants seeds of revelatory truth in our hearts.

He puts us into the right space for miracles to happen by exposing us to the majesty of the Father's loving-kindness.

This issue of potential is absolutely critical both in our own cultivation, and in the development of others. We must expose everyone to the way that the Father sees them so that they can expand into the internal territory that they are exploring.

We must know no one after the flesh, only by their promise in the Spirit. Spirituality in the Kingdom is not about classifying people. There simply is no class system (2 Corinthians 5:16–17).

For example, do not define the poor as people in need of assistance. Instead, define them as having the potential for greatness. Give them creative, nourishing, beautiful, meaningful experiences that unlock who they really are.

Defining poor people as a social burden is a tired, negative mindset. They have as much untapped brilliance as anyone else. Never dismiss the potential of disadvantaged people. Instead, turn that detriment into an asset. Prejudice is un-Christlike. Do not teach people to aim low because of their background. In the Kingdom, all worldly standards are demeaning.

People need hope. A reason to extend themselves, a challenging environment and a supportive framework. We work with God to unlock the identity of all those whom He sends. There is always a way to get from where we are to where we want to be. People need to outgrow their past as they live out their story. We are always rehearsing for our success. Therefore, we need relationships around us that empower us to recognize opportunities as they arise.

Many people, regardless of upbringing are weighed down with self-destructive assumptions about themselves, their life in general, and their own potential and self-worth. We never write people off as a lost cause. We teach people passion for life; also, for their dream and for their development. Passion creates life by giving birth to confidence. People can be fragile flowers living in inhospitable ground. By changing their environment we are effectively transplanting the flower into new soil... *i.e.* new perspective, a new image of themselves. This is at the heart of reframing... giving people new thinking and better language to upgrade their identity.

Personal Notes

How God sees you is how you see yourself. Begin with your potential and move forward. What does that look like to you?

What internal territory are you taking in your present circumstances? Do not define yourself by your current circumstances, instead upgrade your potential.

An Appeal: Anti-Human Trafficking

William Wilberforce has long been one of my favorite heroes. He fought his own government and high society in an epic battle to abolish slavery. He succeeded admirably. In 1833, the British Parliament passed the Slavery Abolition Act which gave freedom to all slaves in the British Empire. Three decades later it also became law in the 13th Amendment to the U.S. Constitution.

Today slavery is back and worse than ever. Former U.S. Secretary of State Condoleeza Rice stated, "defeating human trafficking is a great moral calling of our time." It is a huge business, profitable to the tune of over $30 billion. Almost 30 million people are enslaved by it. Most are children; millions are sex slaves.

We need to raise up a new generation of abolitionists that can counter a worldwide epidemic. Human trafficking is a criminal enterprise that is international. It is sophisticated in its corruptive influence on law enforcement and government officials across the globe.

More slaves are in bondage today than were sold in 400 years of the slave trade that was abolished in the 1800's. Slaves are disposable people—like batteries: once they exhaust their usefulness, they are replaced.

What is required is a relentless pursuit of justice—a refusal to accept a world where one individual can be held as the property of another. For more than three decades I have financed projects around the world aimed at relieving suffering and creating a better quality of life. Fighting against human trafficking is different. It is not a project; it's more of a crusade. I want to affect things at a high level as well as on the ground.

I have a separate account within the ministry where I am setting aside a percentage of profits from all our endeavors to give into this worthy cause. Join us as the Lord leads you, or get involved some way yourself. Do something!

If you wish to donate with your order through Brilliant Book House (please be advised that we are a for-profit company), then send your gift with the notation "Not For Sale" to:

Brilliant Book House
1498 SE Tech Center Pl, Ste 120
Vancouver, WA 98683

Alternatively, if you want a tax credit for your gift, more information and a chance to donate can be found at this website: www.notforsalecampaign.org.

Checks can be made payable to Not for Sale:

270 Capistrano Road, Ste #2
Half Moon Bay, CA 94019

Phone: (650) 560-9990
www.notforsalecampaign.org

With heartfelt thanks,
Graham Cooke

Other Books by Graham Cooke

- A Divine Confrontation… Birth Pangs of the New Church
- Developing Your Prophetic Gifting (Outdated and now out-of-print. It is being replaced by The Prophetic Equipping Series Volumes 1 – 6)
- Permission Granted (co-authored)

The Prophetic Equipping Series:
- Volume 1–Approaching the Heart of Prophecy
- Volume 2–Prophecy and Responsibility
- Volume 3–Prophetic Wisdom

The Being With God Series:
- The Nature of God
- Hiddenness and Manifestation
- Crafted Prayer
- Beholding and Becoming
- Toward a Powerful Inner Life
- The Language of Promise
- God's Keeping Power
- Living in Dependency and Wonder

The Way of the Warrior Series:
- Volume 1–Qualities of a Spiritual Warrior
- Volume 2–Manifesting Your Spirit
- Volume 3–Coming into Alignment

The Wisdom Series:
- Secret Sayings, Hidden Meanings
- Radical Perceptions
- Keys to Brilliant Focus

About The Author

Graham Cooke is a part of the Third Day Movement, an apostolic fellowship of Kingdom builders and church planters around the world. We are a fellowship of permission givers, encouraging each other to experiment with doing church differently, in a way that is more powerful for a post-modern, 21st century culture.

As a partnership of leaders, and a network of churches, ministries and businesses, we are endeavoring to cultivate relationally based encounters that release the priesthood potential of all believers in a given geographic locale or region.

Our passion is to help each individual believer discover their unique identity in Christ and to embrace fully their personal destiny. Graham has been a friend, advisor and speaker within Third Day since 1996 and has co-authored *Permission Granted* with Third Day founder and great friend, Gary Goodell.

Family

Graham is married to Theresa, who has a passion for worship and dance. She loves to be involved in intercession, warfare and setting people free. She cares about injustice and abuse, and has compassion on people who are sick, suffering and disenfranchised.

As a family they have a genealogy that encompasses their immediate household (including a son and daughter by marriage), and also an extended family of Kingdom relatives whom God has joined in Christ.

In the household are three sons, four daughters and four granddaughters. Ben and Seth reside and work in the UK. Ben is a writer, clever, very funny and a passionate lover of music and the movies. Seth is a musician, deep thinker with a caring outlook and a great capacity for mischief. Seth is married to Sara, a lovable, intelligent and very funny woman. They have a daughter Beatrice Cora, a bundle of fun and energy.

Sophie and husband Mark live in Vancouver, WA, and are the Operations Managers for Brilliant Book House. They are at the heart of Graham's publishing company and oversee the marketing, human resources, duplication and distribution of all materials. They are warm hearted, friendly, deeply humorous and very committed to friends and family. They have three daughters. Evelyn (Aug 2006) is delightful; she loves dressing up, dancing and books. Annie (Dec 2008) is loud, funny, determined, unafraid and a developing stuntwoman for the movies! Penny (Feb 2011) is cute, happy and undeterred by her sisters!!

We also have daughters. Alexis is loving, kind and gentle. She is very intuitive and steadfast towards her friends, and a great hairdresser. Alyssa is a very focused, determined woman who is fun loving with a witty sense of humor. She could do anything (!!) and we are watching her develop her real self.

In the extended family line we have three daughters, a son and grandson. Luke and Christa Black with son Moses Grae (Feb 2012) have a special place in our affections, as do Julianne and Megan who both live in Australia. We love this additional part of our family and thank God for them.

Ministry

Graham is a popular conference speaker and is well known for his training programs on the prophetic, spiritual warfare, intimacy and devotional life, leadership, spirituality and the church in transition. He functions as a consultant and freethinker to businesses, churches, and organizations enabling them to develop strategically. He has passion to establish the Kingdom and build prototype churches that can fully reach a post-modern society.

A strong part of Graham's ministry is in producing finances and resources to the poor and disenfranchised in developing countries. He supports many projects specifically for widows, orphans and people in the penal system. He hates abuse of women and works actively against human trafficking and the sex slave trade, including women caught up in prostitution and pornography.

If you would like to invite Graham to minister or speak at an event, please complete the online Ministry Invitation Form at www.brilliantperspectives.com.

If you wish to become a financial partner for the sake of missions and compassionate acts across the nations, please contact his office at office@brilliantperspectives.com, and his administrative assistant will be happy to assist you.

You may contact Graham by writing to:

Graham Cook
865 Cotting Lane, Ste C
Vacaville, CA 95688, USA
www.brilliantperspectives.com

Brilliant Book House

Brilliant Book House is based in Vancouver, WA and is the publishing company founded and directed by Graham Cooke. It is dedicated to producing high-quality Christian resources and teaching materials. Brilliant Book House seeks to equip all of our readers to lead brilliant lives, confidently led by the Holy Spirit into the destiny God has for you.

We believe you have a unique call on your life that can only be found in God. He has something for you that is far beyond your wildest dreams. As you step out into that purpose, we want to stand with you, offering you encouragement, training, and hope for your journey. We want to equip you for what God wants to do in you, and through you. That is our promise to you.

Brilliant is the culmination of a longtime dream of our founder, Graham Cooke. A thinker and a strategist, Graham is also a builder with a particular desire to establish resource churches that are prophetic, progressive, and supernatural. Brilliant Book House is a key part of that call, producing books, journals, MP3s, e-books, DVDs, CDs, and other teaching materials. To see more, please visit www.brilliantbookhouse.com.